MANAGING CRISIS

**Edited by
David Warner and
David Palfreyman**

Open University Press
Maidenhead · Philadelphia

Open University Press
McGraw-Hill Education
McGraw-Hill House
Shoppenhangers Road
Maidenhead
Berkshire
England
SL6 2QL

email: enquiries@openup.co.uk
world wide web: www.openup.co.uk

and
325 Chestnut Street
Philadelphia, PA 19106, USA

First Published 2003

A catalogue record of this book is available from the British Library

ISBN 0 335 21058 9 (pb)   0 335 21059 7 (hb)

Library of Congress Cataloging-in-Publication Data
Managing crisis / edited by David Warner and David Palfreyman.
      p.   cm. – (Managing universities and colleges)
   Includes bibliographical references and index.
   ISBN 0–335–21059–7—ISBN 0–335–21058–9 (pbk.)
   1. Universities and colleges—Great Britain—Business management.
   2. Universities and colleges—Great Britain—Administration.
   I. Warner, David, 1947– II. Palfreyman, David, 1954– III. Series.

   LB2341.93.G7 M36 2003
   378.1′01′0841–dc21
                                                              2002042576
Typeset by RefineCatch Limited, Bungay, Suffolk
Printed and bound in Great Britain by Biddles Ltd, *www.biddles.co.uk*

CONTENTS

FOREWORD

Interest group politics, and media efforts to maintain 24/7 interest in events, have weakened the meaning of crisis. Here today, gone tomorrow. Yet assertions of crisis in higher education abound: governance, recruitment, research support, funding have all from time to time and by different interests been deemed to be in such a state. The focus of this book is not primarily on such contextual crises, but on how individual universities and colleges have managed their own times 'of danger or great difficulty'.

Fortunately, such times are rare. Higher education in the United Kingdom is well managed, well led; no small achievement, given its scale, complexity and the external demands to which it has been exposed. But concatenations of circumstances can threaten financial viability, inhibit recruitment, weaken morale, undermine the effectiveness of governance and management, damage reputation and appear to put institutional futures at risk. Professor Warner, David Palfreyman and their contributors have knowledge and in many cases first-hand experience of such crises and of recovering from them; there is much to learn from their accounts.

Few institutional crises seem to have had long-term effects on institutions' core business of teaching and learning, research and scholarship. Strong leadership, clear priorities and decisive refocusing can produce positive outcomes. However, in the short term, the impact of crises and their aftermath on individuals is often intensely painful, especially when reductions in staff are the only way to balance the books.

To demonstrate awareness of these human costs, to listen to colleagues' concerns, to explain and to justify remedial actions and focus on enhancing morale are not sufficient conditions for success in managing crisis. But they are necessary ones.

William Taylor

NOTES ON CONTRIBUTORS

Roger Brown is Principal of Southampton Institute. Prior to this appointment he was Chief Executive of the Higher Education Quality Council, the then principal quality agency for UK higher education. Roger was previously Head of Research and Strategy at the Committee of Vice-Chancellors and Principals, Chief Executive of the Committee of Directors of Polytechnics and Secretary of the Polytechnics and Colleges Funding Council. He holds visiting professorships at the University of Surrey, Roehampton and the University of East London.

Vanessa Cunningham MBE retired as Senior Executive and Head of the Vice–Chancellor's office at Cardiff University in 1999. In 1987–8 she served the Executive Commission that oversaw the merger of University College Cardiff and the University of Wales Institute of Science and Technology.

Chris Duke is currently Professor of Regional Partnership and Learning, and Director of Community and Regional Partnership, at RMIT University (formerly Royal Melbourne Institute of Technology). He is also part-time Associate Director of Higher Education for the (England and Wales) National Institute of Adult and Continuing Education. Chris was recently Professor and Director of Continuing Education at the University of Auckland and before that President of the University of Western Sydney Nepean.

Brian Fender (Sir) was Chief Executive of the Higher Education Funding Council for England from 1995 to 2001. Prior to that he was Vice-Chancellor of Keele University (1985–95) and Associate Director and Director of the Institut Laue-Langevin in Grenoble, France (1980–5), and before that he taught inorganic chemistry at Oxford University. Brian is currently President of the National Foundation for Educational Research, a non-executive director of BTG plc and a director of Higher Aims Ltd. He was knighted in 1999 for his services to higher education.

Roderick Floud is Provost of London Guildhall University. As an economic historian he previously taught at University College London, Birkbeck and Stanford. Roderick has been a member of the Council of the Economic and Social Research Council, is a member of the Council of Gresham College and is President of Universities UK for the period 2001–3.

Lucy Hodges edits the *Independent*'s weekly education supplement and writes about higher education for that paper. She has been in educational journalism for several decades, having been education correspondent of *The Times* and the *Evening Standard*. For five years Lucy was the American correspondent of *The Times Higher Education Supplement*, writing about US higher education for a British audience.

Marion McClintock is Academic Registrar and Clerk to the Council at the University of Lancaster. Her first publication on the development of Lancaster, *Quest for Innovation*, was produced in 1974.

David Palfreyman is the Bursar and a Fellow of New College, Oxford. Prior to this appointment he worked at the Universities of Warwick and Liverpool. With David Warner, he has edited *Higher Education Management*, *The State of UK Higher Education* (both published by Open University Press) and *Higher Education Law*. David has also co-authored *Oxford and the Decline of the Collegiate Tradition*.

Adrian Perry was formerly Principal of Lambeth College and prior to that was Principal of Parson Cross College in Sheffield. He is a director of the London Central Learning and Skills Council, sits on the boards overseeing Lambeth's New Deal and Education Action Zone, and was founding Chair of the South London Learning Partnership.

William Ritchie has been the Vice-Chancellor of the University of Lancaster since 1995, and was previously Vice-Principal of the University of Aberdeen. He is a member of the Fulbright Commission and of the Board of the National Maritime Museum (Greenwich).

Peter Scott is the Vice-Chancellor of Kingston University and a member of the Board of the Higher Education Funding Council for England. Prior to this appointment in 1998, he was Pro-Vice-Chancellor, Professor of Education and Director of the Centre for Policy Studies in Education at the University of Leeds. Peter was Editor of *The Times Higher Education Supplement* from 1976 to 1992.

Brian Smith (Sir) was formerly Vice-Chancellor of Cardiff University, and prior to that was Master of St Catherine's College, Oxford. He was knighted in 1999 for his services to higher education.

William Taylor (Sir) was formerly Director of the University of London Institute of Higher Education, Vice-Chancellor of the

University of Hull and during the 1990s interim Vice-Chancellor of Huddersfield and Thames Valley Universities. He was knighted in 1990 for his services to higher education.

David Warner is the Principal of Swansea Institute of Higher Education, having previously worked at the Universities of Warwick, East Anglia and Central England in Birmingham. With David Palfreyman, he is the joint commissioning editor of the Open University Press series *Managing Universities and Colleges*, in which this volume appears.

LIST OF ABBREVIATIONS

ALF	average level of funding
APR	age participation rate
ASN	additional student numbers
AUT	Association of University Teachers
BSE	bovine spongiform encephalopathy
CAE	college of advanced education
CEO	chief executive officer
CLP	City of London Polytechnic
CNAA	Council for National Academic Awards
CUIN	Cardiff University Innovation Network
CVCP	Committee of Vice-Chancellors and Principals (now Universities UK)
DES	Department of Education and Science
DfE	Department for Education
DfEE	Department for Education and Employment
DfES	Department for Education and Skills
DTI	Department of Trade and Industry
EU	European Union
FE	further education
FEFC	Further Education Funding Council
FEI	further education institution
FHE	further and higher education
FHEIs	further and higher education institutions
FMD	foot and mouth disease
FTE	full-time equivalent (students)
GWS	Greater Western Sydney
HE	higher education
HEC	higher education corporation

HEFCE	Higher Education Funding Council for England
HEFCW	Higher Education Funding Council for Wales
HEI	higher education institution
HMI	Her Majesty's Inspectorate
HEQC	Higher Education Quality Council
ILEA	Inner London Education Authority
IT	information technology
ITT	initial teacher training
LEA	local education authority
LGU	London Guildhall University
LSC	Learning and Skills Council
MASN	maximum aggregate student number
MP	Member of Parliament
NAO	National Audit Office
NATFHE	National Association of Teachers in Further and Higher Education
NERC	Natural Environment Research Council
NHS	National Health Service
NTEU	National Tertiary Education Union
NUS	National Union of Students
OECD	Organization for Economic Co-operation and Development
OFSTED	Office for Standards in Education
PGCE	postgraduate certificate in education
PwC	PricewaterhouseCoopers
QAA	Quality Assurance Agency
RAE	Research Assessment Exercise
RSA	Royal Society of Arts
SCOP	Standing Conference of Principals
SIHE	Swansea Institute of Higher Education
SRHE	Society for Research into Higher Education
SWOT	strengths, weaknesses, opportunities and threats (analysis)
TEC	training and enterprise council
THES	*The Times Higher Education Supplement*
TTA	Teacher Training Agency
TQA	teaching quality assessment
TVU	Thames Valley University
UCAS	Universities and Colleges Admissions Service
UCC	University College Cardiff
UCE	University of Central England in Birmingham
UCL	University College London
UGC	Universities Grants Committee (now defunct)
UNE	University of New England (Australia)

UNS	United National System (Australia)
USS	universities superannuation scheme
UWIST	University of Wales Institute of Science and Technology
UWE	University of the West of England
UWS	University of Western Sydney
VC	vice-chancellor
VCSAG	vice-chancellor's strategic advisory group

1

SETTING THE SCENE
David Warner and David Palfreyman

Genesis of the book

The 20-volume *Managing Universities and Colleges* series in which this volume appears aims to provide a set of guides to good practice. The editors' interest in the subject of crisis was aroused as the result of a chance remark made by a senior professional colleague who mused that, while there was no reluctance to write about the management of change in higher education, in contrast no one seemed keen to put pen to paper on the nitty-gritty issues that really mattered: namely, how to turn a failing higher education institution (HEI) round and how to manage a failing member of staff. This latter issue, which besets every HEI (although we all usually prefer to sweep it under the carpet), remains a problem too far and perhaps others will turn their attention to it in due course (see the recent volume in this series: Pat Partington on *Managing Staff Development*, 2003). The editors, however, in their innocence believed that, in relation to the former issue of institutional rather than personal failure, they could readily convince a team of highly quali-fied and appropriate senior staff to write a series of case studies under the generic title of *The Failing Institution*. They were wrong: almost all of the initial contacts declined – usually graciously, but nevertheless firmly.

It was an exchange of correspondence with Sir William Taylor, the doyen of 'HEI company doctors' and the author of the Foreword, that highlighted the editors' mistake. Our working title was far too negative and implied a current and continuing state of affairs. Sir William suggested the far more challenging and acceptable title of *Managing Crisis*. However, even with this new title, it proved impossible to gain contributions on some *causes célèbres*. The reasons given were varied, but bear consideration. They include:

- A state of sheer fatigue still existing among all of the key participants.
- A desire not to reopen old wounds, which, at the time of contact, appeared to be healing, although no one was confident that there would not remain at least a lot of unsightly scar tissue.
- A belief that all the relevant facts were already in the public arena and that reflective analysis would not add anything to them.
- The problem of existing legal actions and the possibility that new ones might result from any injudicious words.
- The argument from affront, namely that 'crisis' is a subjective term and 'I never thought that my institution was in one.'
- A desire not to be seen as blowing one's own trumpet and claiming the turnaround of the institution as primarily due to the efforts of one person: it appears that further and higher education (FHE) does not readily support the cult of the personality!

Contents and contributors

In the light of the above hurdles, the editors are delighted to have gathered together such a distinguished group of contributors. Their names, positions and experience speak for themselves. The brief for the core UK case study chapters of the book was simple: each author was asked to provide a little background about the FHEI concerned; to identify what were (possibly still are) the problems, how the problems came to light and what has been done (or is being done) to put the problems aright; and to speculate a little about the future. The result is seven very important 'stories', each of which is worth studying in its own right and, at the same time, contributes to the broader picture.

The international chapter provided the editors with a considerable headache, although not because of its quality. Chris Duke took as his remit the whole structure of the book and included both references to the literature and general observations. The editors hesitated: should the chapter be hacked about or should it be left to stand as a single, coherent contribution? This was the dilemma. After much soul searching and correspondence, the editors decided to leave the chapter as it was originally written and, therefore, must crave the indulgence of the reader about any possible repetition. The decision was a hard one to make and was in no way influenced by Chris's gentle hint that an Australian vice-chancellor (VC) had only just resigned over a 20-year-old plagiarism!

FHE crises, especially those having a financial dimension (and which do not?), are clearly a responsibility (or at least a concern) of the funding councils. Sir Brian Fender's chapter, therefore, is of particular interest as it shows exactly what goes on, and the responses that are made, within these 'shadowy bodies' when things go wrong. FHE institutions are legally independent bodies, but this status, which we all cherish, also entails the right to go bankrupt. How far will funding councils go to solve a crisis? Will they inevitably become planning as well as funding bodies? Will politicians allow the bankruptcy of a FHEI? The concluding chapter by Peter Scott provides one of the best thinkers and writers in the world on higher education with a wide canvass on which to work. He has not disappointed us.

At this juncture, it must be pointed out that, irrespective of his or her position (or former position) in the organization concerned, each author has written as an individual and in no way claims to speak on behalf of anyone else, or on behalf of any institution or body.

FHE crises in perspective

There is a commonly held belief in UK government circles (and probably in the business world as well) that further and higher education institutions are badly managed by untrained amateurs at most levels of the organization. Consequently, when a crisis surfaces in FHE, usually brought to light as a result of the very elaborate and multilayered audit regimes from which the system benefits (and this last term is not used in an ironic sense), then the media, even the relatively gentle education media, immediately look for scandal and begin a feeding frenzy. Yet what is the incidence of *real* crises in the sector? And especially compared with recent mismanagement and misgovernance scandals on a truly massive scale (Barings, Marconi, Equitable Life, Independent Insurance, Railtrack, Enron, Tyco, Worldcom . . .).

There are at the time of writing 171[1] HE institutions in the UK and approximately 500[2] FE institutions, including sixth form colleges. During the past decade, despite arguably severe underfunding, there have been no more than a dozen reported crises and only about half of these have generated National Audit Office reports. On an annual basis, this means that only 0.2 per cent of HEIs are affected or, to put it another way, 99.8 per cent have a relatively clean bill of health. In comparison with the private sector (as noted above) or even central and local government (the expensive mishandling of BSE and FMD, the collapse of education services in some London boroughs, the electoral gerrymandering within Westminster Council . . .), this is a very low figure. There may be individual FHE crises, but the sector is certainly not in crisis. And it is far better managed than it is ever given credit for.

Yet undeniably there are crises of varying degrees of drama and severity, and, moreover, 'crisis' can take many forms for a FHEI: the fires at City University and York University; sudden financial melt-down at Bristol University and at Lancaster; a slow loss of financial control at Edinburgh, Aberdeen or UCL; the strategic collapse of Cardiff or Thames Valley; a 'no confidence' vote in the VC's leader-ship at Goldsmiths or Portsmouth; the 'overtrading' at Southampton IHE or Swansea IHE as overseas franchising went badly wrong; the ramifications of the closure of a single academic department, as at Birmingham; a bungled IT project at Cambridge; massive staff cuts at Aston, Bradford and Salford; student underrecruitment at De Montfort; media exposé of 'places for donations' at Oxford; student occupation of key buildings at Warwick; legal wranglings over campus 'free speech' at Liverpool University; sacking the VC at Glasgow Caledonian; 'soap'-style academic squabbling over many years within a department at Swansea University; student litigation over the quality of 'the learning experience' at Wolverhampton; the impounding by the police of an art book under the Obscene Publications Act and the potential prosecution of the VC at UCE; dangerous failings in laboratory safety at Imperial; media attention over deficient teaching of a single module at Liverpool John Moores; a student raped on her year abroad claiming negligence on the part of St Andrew's in despatching her to Odessa; campus damage from a mini-hurricane at Sussex University . . . Is *your* FHEI next?

The management theory and literature: A brief review

Most textbooks on organizational psychology, on strategic manage-ment or on the management of change will have an index entry for items such as 'risk assessment management', 'crisis planning and management', 'disaster recovery', 'contingency management' or 'managing turbulence': see, for example, Thompson (2001: Chapter 23) for a neat section on risk management, on crisis avoidance and on crisis/disaster recovery within a comprehensive management strategy textbook. There will also be an endless flow of 'one-minute-manager' guides for dealing with crises, each offering tick-lists and calming thoughts (for example, Jay 2001). A somewhat superior version of that genre is Gottschalk (2002), along with Mitroff (2000) and also Harrington *et al.* (1996). At the other end of the (not very wide) intellectual scale are books and articles by management academics (for instance, *Harvard Business Review on Crisis Management* 2000, and *Harvard Business Review on Turnarounds* 2001). Websites offering crisis management information (and indeed services) are:

- www.crisisnavigator.org;
- www.crisisexperts.com ('Institute for Crisis Management').

Chapter 24 in *Higher Education Law* (Palfreyman and Warner 2002) is on 'risk management and insurance', and we refer to the 'Active Risk Management in Education' project at www.bristol.ac.uk/armed, and to HEFCE's *Risk Management in Further and Higher Education*. For more on *legal* risk avoidance, risk control, risk transfer and risk retention policies at US HEIs, see Kaplin and Lee (1995: 137–42).

The deceptively neat (and even naive) academic theory is that:

- one carefully assesses the risk faced by the enterprise;
- one takes prudent steps to avoid or minimize some risks if possible, or to shift them elsewhere (typically via appropriate insurance cover);
- one prepares detailed emergency and recovery plans to deal with risks that are retained (often whether one likes it or not);
- one implements those plans as necessary in 'disaster/crisis management mode';
- later one reviews the plans to see if they worked (while also, of course, constantly updating them anyway).

Practical reality, however, is rarely as neat and tidy as management theory, as even the best resourced and supposedly prepared organizations can discover. Moreover, 'crisis' may be not in the form of a sudden disaster (fire, key personnel dying, equipment failure, IT virus etc.) needing a short and sharp management response over a fixed period or in one locality, but in the form of a steady corporate-wide decline over time needing sustained management effort to achieve a turnaround (if indeed one is at all possible). Air crashes, the Titanic sinking, pollution incidents, product contamination, nuclear power plant accidents, the fraudulent trading losses at Allied Irish Bank or Barings are the 'sudden disaster' type of crisis; Enron, Marconi, Equitable Life, Railtrack and Independent Insurance are examples of systemic corporate failure, as also with University College Cardiff (see Shattock 1994: Chapter 6) or the still unfolding University of Cambridge CAPSA IT fiasco (see Palfreyman and Warner 2002: 95–7; see also the OxCHEPS occasional paper on HEI governance).

The US Institute for Crisis Management defines a crisis as: 'A significant business disruption which stimulates extensive news media coverage. The resulting public scrutiny will affect the organization's normal operations and also could have a political, legal, financial, and governmental impact on its business.' The advice of crisis consultants (such as Douglas Hearle) is that the corporate executives need: to act *fast*; to be the ones to reveal facts *first*; to spell it all out *fully*; to be *factual*; to be *frank* and *forthright*; to remain *focused*; to ensure the appropriate *facilities* are available; to seek *feedback*; to be prepared to express *feelings* and compassion to any people hurt. There may well, however, be a conflict between the legal advisors warning 'Say little. Admit nothing', and the PR folk advising 'Come clean. Take the initiative. Assert control.' Integrity and credibility will favour the latter, but remember that your insurers may not be too happy if you admit liability. On the HEI's external relations strategy see Albrighton and Thomas (2001).

While the fire at City University may be an example of the former type of disaster-crisis, this book is more about the generalized-crisis that needs to be addressed by 'a turnaround', by a process of 'transformational change'. The management literature suggests that the features of such a change process include:

- an emphasis on open and honest communication;
- a willingness to listen to employees and draw upon their expertise;
- offering constant feedback;
- setting conservative, limited goals at first; only later, and building on initial modest success, try more aggressive goals; start small and win often;
- experiment, and learn from failure;
- constantly review, revise and enhance;
- provide staff with a vision, a manifesto;
- act as a team, as a coalition;
- win people over; don't demean and humiliate (unless you think life is best lived and HEIs best managed on a Hobbesian basis of being 'nasty, brutish and short'!).

That said, the HE manager seeking profound guidance from the management literature[3] is in for a disappointment. The ticklists *may* help in a crisis; but what passes for academic thinking about longer-term institutional and cultural change can be rather banal, unstructured, not analytical and overly anecdotal (with an undue emphasis on the Great Man who alone turned it all around). Perhaps the best general reads are Kanter's *The Change Masters* (1983) and Kay's *Foundations of Corporate Success* (1993); see also on corporate culture and strategic planning for HEIs Chapters 2 and 3 of Warner and Palfreyman (1996), Watson (2000) and Duke (2002); Keller (1983) too is worth looking at. As already noted, Thompson (2001) is a good general text on strategic management, with plenty of flow charts on the planning process, SWOT analysis, the product strength matrix etc. That said, there really is no substitute for common sense, tempered with a little managerial humility.

So why do organizations face crises? There is little we as HEIs can do to avoid weather or other natural disasters; we all will have an emergency plan and a crisis recovery plan, along with insurance and the hope that the 1960s flat roofs are sufficiently well maintained so as not to leak in a storm. But some organizations are *crisis prone*, with poor strategy, poor control systems, cost-cutting leading to neglect, failure to learn from experience, a 'group think'/'yes-man' culture, no holistic vision, poor internal communication ... Thus, the crisis evolves gradually; no one scans the environment to check for threats and challenges; there is complacency or even self-delusion, 'group-think' and denial. Sadly, the HEI has no monopoly on clear, rational thinking, nor any immunity from developing a short-sighted bunker mentality, as the following case studies depressingly and convincingly show. But one *can* learn from the experience (and mistakes) of others.

Notes

1 This figure varies from year to year as, on the one hand, mergers between HEIs reduce the total and, on the other, it is increased by new institutions gaining HE status under the terms of the 1992 Further and Higher Education Act.
2 This total too is variable, but usually downwards as a result of mergers.
3 For some useful case studies on managing corporate crisis in the private sector see Monks and Minow (2001: Chapter 6). On the huge and broad issue of 'management', the sensible starting point is 'What is management?' (Magretta 2002), and after that the supply of management books, theoretical and practical, good and bad, is, of course, endless.

2

CRISIS AT CARDIFF
Brian Smith and Vanessa Cunningham

Introduction

Cardiff University, created in 1988 through the merger of two neighbouring university colleges, has rapidly established itself as one of the UK's leading research universities. *The Times Higher Education Supplement* on 11 January 2002 described it as 'riding on a wave of confidence following spectacular research assessment exercise results'. Yet at the time of the merger neither of the two parent institutions was in the front rank of universities, and one was facing bankruptcy at the centre of a widely publicized financial scandal. This chapter first describes that crisis, and goes on to outline how it was initially resolved. The remainder of the case study examines the actions taken by Cardiff since merger to achieve the success it currently enjoys, and speculates on the extent to which the crisis of the mid-1980s has influenced both the corporate culture at Cardiff and the UK higher education sector as a whole.

Crisis? What crisis?

'If you want to bring about major and rapid change in an organization, first create a crisis.' This familiar advice might easily spring to mind when the financial affairs of University College Cardiff (UCC) in the mid-1980s are mentioned. It is certainly applicable to the events of the astonishing year 1987–8, which ended with the legal merger of UCC and its neighbour the University of Wales Institute of Science and Technology (UWIST). But it has little relevance to the immediately preceding period. Indeed, in retrospect it can be seen that one of the most bizarre aspects of the whole affair was that, while alarmed outsiders such as the University Grants Committee (UGC) were calling on UCC to take urgent corrective action, those insiders most responsible continued until a very late stage to deny that anything was amiss. The extent to which, in 1986 and 1987, senior managers, let alone the College Council, ever fully understood the magnitude of the difficulties that faced UCC is still a matter for debate.

The first hint to the sector that there might be problems at Cardiff came in a short item on page 3 of *The Times Higher Education Supplement* on 7 February 1986. It began:

Cardiff books investigated

A firm of accountants has been called in by the Department of Education and Science to investigate the financial position of University College, Cardiff. Price Waterhouse have been asked to verify whether the College's estimates of how it will clear its £3.5 million accumulated debt are accurate. Dr Cecil Bevan, the principal, said accountants would be looking at specific matters relating to the College's financial position ... He said the DES had called in the auditors 'after certain alarmist noises had been made'.

That a university institution could be on the brink of bankruptcy was an unprecedented event within the UK higher education sector. The chairman of the University Grants Committee, Sir Peter Swinnerton-Dyer, and the permanent secretary at the Department of Education and Science (DES), Sir David Hancock, had been struggling for months to persuade the college to put its financial house in order. Sir David, the accounting officer for the universities, remained dissatisfied with the realism of the college's responses; hence his decision in January 1986 to take the unprecedented step of appointing the accountants Price Waterhouse to report on the state of UCC's finances, current and future. The convention that the UGC, by operating as a buffer between government and the universities, would protect the autonomy of the institutions to which it distributed public funding had been well and truly breached. Until the Cardiff crisis, the UGC had operated in accordance with the policy set out in its letter of guidance to universities for the 1972–7 quinquennial planning period:

The Committee in framing their advice to universities have to try to meet the needs of the country as a whole, while taking account of any requirements laid down by the Government of the day. At the same time they hold strongly that within this framework each individual university institution should be left to manage its own affairs with the minimum of detailed instructions.

(Quoted in Shattock 1994: 114)[1]

By the time the crisis had been resolved, the fate of University College Cardiff had become a topic of debate within Downing Street itself.

Price Waterhouse reported in April 1986. In the words of Michael Shattock (1994: 116):

> The Price Waterhouse report confirmed the UGC's worst fears . . . It forecast a further deficit of £1.184 million in 1986–87, a cumulative deficit in that year of £5.119 million and a bank overdraft of up to £5.315 million. It was extremely critical of Cardiff's approach to financial planning and the optimistic assumptions on which it was based.

The college's response was pained and indignant. It challenged Price Waterhouse's figures, claiming that its plans were realistic and that it expected a surplus of £1.633 million in 1986–7. Its counter-assessment of its financial position, writes Shattock (1994: 117), 'represented a flight from reality on the part of the College's senior administrators and the College Council'. In the months that followed, the DES continued to press the college to submit monthly monitoring reports to the UGC, and also to draw up financial and academic plans that would reflect the increasingly gloomy prospects that were being forecast for the university sector as a whole. The reports were never made, and the plans, when at last they arrived, were over-optimistic. With the college management apparently incapable of facing up to the seriousness of its financial position, no significant remedial action was taken and the crisis continued to deepen. In early February 1987 Sir David Hancock applied the ultimate sanction. He informed Sir William Crawshay, chairman of UCC's council, that the college would receive no more instalments of recurrent grant unless its finance committee agreed to the appointment of two external teams, one accountable to the UGC and one appointed by the college itself, to take a grip on UCC's finances and to draw up recovery plans. With the prospect of being unable to pay its staff at the end of the month, the college had no option but to agree. The UGC team comprised financial managers from other universities and was headed by Michael Shattock; UCC appointed the accountants Ernst and Whinney. All these professionals, working together as a single visiting team, rapidly produced a succession of financial recovery plans, all involving very severe reductions in numbers of academic and academic-related staff (between 125 to 142, according to the scenario selected), together with heavy cuts of at least 15 per cent in all other expenditure heads. Recurrent grant payments were restored in March, but in the months that followed the UGC received little evidence that the college was capable of reorganizing itself, and in particular of shedding staff, to the necessary extent. Bankruptcy continued to loom. The bursar resigned; so did the chairman of council and the treasurer.

What caused these dramatic and unprecedented events? Those who experienced them are not unanimous about the reasons, but they do all agree that the strong personality of Dr Cecil (Bill) Bevan, the college's principal from 1966 to 1987, was a crucial factor. Dr Bevan's story has something of Greek tragedy about it. At the University of Ibadan, Nigeria, he had been a highly successful deputy vice-chancellor. He saw in Cardiff the potential to become a great university and recognized the need for expansion on a large scale. His strong will and powers of leadership are evident in his portrait by David Griffiths, which dominates Cardiff's council chamber to this day. The relatively prosperous early years of his incumbency, when he began to bring his grand vision into being, are recalled by staff who were there as happy and exciting times. By the end of the 1970s, full-time student numbers had increased from 3304 in 1969–70 to 5474 in 1979–80, academic staff had grown from 411 to 580 and the college estate had been much enlarged.

But for universities the wind was beginning to change to a much chillier blast. Prys Morgan (1997: 158), in his history of the University of Wales, states: 'It is said that at the first signs of cuts and economies in 1974, Bevan's slogan was "We want to expand like hell".' In 1981 the UGC was obliged to reduce recurrent grants and impose cuts in student numbers. Most universities recognized the need to reduce expenditure and took steps to do so, many facing far more stringent cuts than those imposed on UCC. Typically, UCC resisted the advice to cut costs, preferring to rely mainly on a plan to increase fee income from overseas students. But the college was overreliant on the Nigerian market. In none of the first four years of the 1980s had enrolments from that country fallen below 30 per cent of the total number of overseas students. Unfortunately, a military coup in Lagos at the end of December 1983 led to new exchange control rules, and numbers of Nigerian students at Cardiff fell rapidly, from 254 in 1983–4 to 68 in 1986–7. And while other institutions were freezing vacant posts, UCC continued to make appointments. When the single chairholder in metallurgy retired in 1983, the college appointed *two* professors to succeed him, in a direct challenge to the UGC's advice that the subject should be run down at Cardiff.

Dr Bevan was convinced that somehow Cardiff would weather the storm, and saw it as his duty to resist the repeated demands of the UGC for details of the college's plans for retrenchment. In 1984, as recalled by John Goodwin, the confrontation intensified:

> Principal Bevan's 'hands on' approach to life was perhaps best typi-fied by his infamous 1984 'k.b.o.' letter to the University Grants Committee. The UGC had sought reams of information from all universities on prospects and proposals, and most institutions had responded at length. In the Principal's office a very brief response was prepared. Its key message was phrased in the identical words used by Winston Churchill when asked how he intended to prosecute the war: 'keep buggering on'.
>
> (Goodwin and Cunningham 2001: 62)

From the point of view of the UGC, some action was now inevit-able, but by whom it should be taken was debatable. There were no precedents for intervention by the UGC, nor by the University of Wales, since the UGC dealt directly with and funded the university's member colleges as if they were independent institutions. In the words of Prys Morgan (1997: 159), 'no real defences existed in the college or University to limit the plans of a principal who believed it was possible to spend his way out of trouble.' Dr Bevan was used to having things all his own way. 'Rules are for fools,' he was often heard to say. Such was the power of his personality that senior adminis-trators were either unwilling or unable to gainsay him, and could provide neither adequate day-to-day financial management nor credible forecasts. The principal saw the job of the college's finance department as supplying the funds he needed to realize his visions of expansion. 'Bursar: some creative accounting if you please' was a typical endorsement on a request sent to him for financial support. Assertive internal counteraction might in theory have averted external intervention, since on paper the usual constitutional checks and balances were in place. But in fact the lay-dominated governing bodies of the college, its court and council, appeared wholly supportive of their charismatic principal. Only the academic staff seemed to recognize the collision course upon which the college had embarked; at successive meetings of the senate they expressed their growing disquiet. On 9 December 1986 the senate recorded its lack of confidence in the central financial management of the college. The following month, and in the absence of the principal, a motion was carried 'that senate has no confidence in the principal'. At the next meeting (17 February 1987) the principal was once more in the chair, and the senate was reminded that he held that office under college statutes. Dr Bevan withdrew while members discussed the position. The deadpan style of the minutes cannot disguise what must have been a sensational confrontation. The record continues:

> After a discussion *it was resolved* that the Principal be asked not to exercise his right to chair meetings of the Senate. Having been informed of this resolution by the Deputy Principal (Humanities) the Principal returned to the meeting and informed the Senate that he intended to exercise his right to chair its meetings.

He was not to exercise that right for much longer. In March 1987 he was granted sabbatical leave, to run until his retirement date of 30 September 1987, one of the many (often the ablest and most energetic) who left the college in that year. Indeed, one of the saddest ironies of this sad story is that the price, when finally paid, for refusing to face facts turned out to be the loss to UCC of more than 140 academic staff.

It would be wrong to give the impression that UCC did nothing about its financial crisis. Though the college seemed to be unable to grasp the need to reduce its staffing bill on anything like the necessary scale, numerous committees, task forces, working parties and ginger groups were set up during 1986 and 1987 to identify areas in which economies could be made, and some useful if relatively minor savings were secured. An extremely generous early retirement scheme was eventually offered to staff in June 1986; fortunately, there were few takers. But to many, both in Cardiff and in London, the most obvious and satisfactory solution appeared to be a merger between UCC and its sister college the University of Wales Institute of Science and Technology (UWIST). Geographically the two colleges were very close; philosophically they certainly were not. Prys Morgan (1997: 157) writes:

> The impasse was caused by the mutual suspicion of the councils and staffs of the two great institutions in Cardiff ... glaring at each other over the Temple of Peace and the Welsh National War Memorial in Cathays Park, and also by the mutual incompatibility of the two principals.

In 1976 it became clear that no public funding would be provided to enable UWIST to fulfil its ambitious plan to move to a greenfield site elsewhere in Wales. The UGC began to put increasing pressure on all three Cardiff institutions (the Welsh National School of Medicine was the third) to plan their capital developments in common. From 1981 the UGC was urging UCC and UWIST to unite, holding out as reward the prospect of new buildings for a single Faculty of Engineering. But formal progress towards merger was halting. Discussions started in 1982, were broken off by UWIST in 1983 and started again in 1984. While UCC continued to express strong commitment to amalgamation, UWIST was perturbed by the growing gap between its own estimates of UCC's future finances and the far rosier prospects held out by that college's representatives. UWIST, younger, smaller and with fewer areas of academic distinction, was a tight ship, run by its principal, Dr (now Sir) Aubrey Trotman-Dickenson, on lines very different from the regime across the park. Thanks to realistic financial planning and firm control over a key element – the salary bill for permanent academic staff – UWIST had weathered the cuts of the early 1980s well. The chairman of the UGC described Dr Trotman-Dickenson as 'one of the very best financial managers that any university or college has'. On the back of the proverbial envelope he could show that UCC's finances were spiralling out of control, but attempts by the UWIST negotiators to discuss the issue were met with indignation. Throughout the 'on–off' merger talks and the financial crisis at UCC, a joint group was steadily taking forward the planning of the UGC-funded joint engineering development – a prize that neither side could contemplate giving up. Yet at the same time UWIST, hovering anxiously in the wings as UCC headed inexorably for bankruptcy, was determined not to accept any merger terms that involved the sacrifice of UWIST staff on what it saw as the altar of UCC's profligacy.

By the summer of 1987 it was time for intervention at the highest level. The Secretary of State for Wales, Nicholas Edwards (now Lord Crickhowell), was active in putting together a rescue plan. 'Whatever other arguments might be valid', he recalls, 'the thought of having several thousand academics and students thrown onto the streets of Cardiff during a general election campaign was clearly not attractive' (Crickhowell 1999: 104). But the Prime Minister, Mrs Thatcher, had decreed in a minute circulated throughout Whitehall that there should be no question of bailing out UCC. Following a cabinet meeting, Edwards approached her:

> 'Prime Minister, this is not a moment when you want problems – you want solutions. John MacGregor [Chief Secretary to the Treasury], Kenneth Baker [Secretary of State for Education] and I have just worked out a solution to the problem of University College, Cardiff. Can I have your consent?' She looked at me with well-justified suspicion that the solution was not of the kind indicated in her recent minute . . . 'Oh, very well,' said the

Prime Minister. 'Thank you,' I replied. She had not seen the proposed solution but had trusted us enough.

(Crickhowell 1999: 105)

The 'solution' offered to UCC by the UGC in May 1987 was generous: a grant of £5 million to enable it to shed the necessary number of academic and academic-related staff by the end of March 1988, and a further £4.4 million as an interest-free loan to reduce the college's overdraft. (The loan was to be repaid from sales of capital assets.) But stark conditions were attached: the immediate replacement of Dr Bevan by a successor acceptable to UWIST, and an irrevocable commitment to merger by both institutions. A liaison group, chaired by a senior civil servant, Sir Idwal Pugh, rapidly produced a legally binding agreement to merge in 1988. It was sealed by both councils on 21 July 1987. By that date, Dr Bevan and all but one of his remaining senior administrators had already departed from UCC. Dr Trotman-Dickenson took over as UCC's last principal for the final year of the college's existence, with the assurance that he would serve as the first principal of the new merged institution. An executive commission, representing both institutions and chaired by Sir Donald Walters, took up the formidable challenge of bringing about merger within a matter of months.

A new start

The executive commission met for the first time on 28 July 1987. The majority of members were from UWIST, including the chair, principal-designate and secretary. There were five members of UCC's council. UCC had had to agree 'to ratify all decisions of the executive commission taken within its powers and functions', and there could be no doubt as to which institution was in the driving seat. Yet from a very early stage the members of the commission demonstrated a striking ability to put past differences behind them and a shared desire to concentrate on building for the future. The following abbreviated list shows some of the formidable tasks that lay ahead of them. The agreement of 21 July 1987 required them to:

• Draft, submit to the Privy Council and secure approval for a charter and statutes upon which to establish the new institution on 31 March 1988. (In the event, this target date was shifted, first to 31 August 1988 and eventually to 26 September 1988.)

- Prepare, maintain and implement a financial plan and an academic plan for UCC and for the new institution, coordinated with existing UWIST plans.
- Eliminate UCC's financial deficit and manage its finances to the satisfaction of the UGC.
- Decide on the number and identity of members of the staff of UCC whose services would have to be dispensed with.
- Manage and control the real property and buildings of both parent colleges.
- Draw up ordinances and regulations for the new institution.

In addition to the preparations for merger, the routine management of the two parent institutions had to continue, including meetings of committees, senates and councils. To assist the executive commission, a management team, with limited delegated powers, met weekly. It comprised the principal, the registrar and two members of the academic staff from each college.

The most urgent task for the executive commission was to convince the UGC that affairs at Cardiff were now under control and thus to secure the release of promised funds. By mid-September 1987 a brief initial academic and financial plan (AFP1) had been sent to the UGC, outlining for the new institution a faculty and departmental structure, with associated student numbers for each, long-term permanent staff targets and a financial strategy. The financial plan was predicated on the basis that in 1989–90 the portion of the academic staff salary bill deriving from UCC would cost less than £11 million. Therefore, in those early months, achieving the necessary staff reductions while maintaining commitments to students was given highest priority. It was necessary, as a precaution, to give notice to the Association of University Teachers (AUT) that compulsory redundancies might be required. But on 6 December 1987 the executive commission was relieved to be able to announce that sufficient commitments to depart voluntarily had been secured, and in mid-February 1988 a full academic and financial plan (AFP2) was despatched to the UGC. By this time, headships of all the departments of the new college had been decided; the two law departments had united, and several departments from both colleges had already been brought together to form the Cardiff Business School. AFP2 also contained an individual plan for each of the 29 departments that would exist on charter day. (UWIST had had 15 departments, UCC more than 40.) This evidence was sufficient to induce the UGC and DES by the end of March 1988 to release the promised funding 'to facilitate the creation of a new university institution in Cardiff'.[2] The actual sums were

- £4.957 million for UCC premature retirement and redundancy compensation.
- £4.402 million repayable grant in respect of UCC's accumulated liabilities as at 31 July 1987.
- £1.733 million: essential backlog maintenance in UCC.

The crucial part played by this pump-priming funding in achieving a successful merger cannot be overstated.

The creation of a single administration was another task of great urgency. Key administrative staff were given parallel appointments in both colleges, in anticipation of the senior posts they would hold in the new institution. Wherever possible, administrative divisions were physically merged and run 'as one' before the legal date of amalgamation. Similar arrangements were made for the library and the computing service. The two students' unions already shared a building and were keen to unite formally; other accommodation problems were much less easy to solve. In parallel with the UGC-funded development for engineering at Newport Road, a five-year physical restructuring programme began in order to rationalize and integrate the two neighbouring but separate estates. Meanwhile, there was a financial allocation system for the new college to be devised (something of a novelty for UCC), a prospectus to be published, a corporate image to develop and a streamlined committee system to design – all within a year. Along with all this came much 'fire-fighting' activity arising from UCC's financial collapse, since it was essential to ensure that academic programmes to which students had signed up in good faith were kept going, and that the personal positions of individual staff were not overlooked when new structures were put in place.

In tackling this huge range of work, the executive commission had several advantages. The chair was widely experienced and able, and the principal was a first-class financial manager with a remarkable grasp of detail. Furthermore, the commission's secretary, Professor Mick Bruton, was a strategic thinker with an academic background in planning. He had been head of the department of town planning before taking up the post of deputy principal and registrar of UWIST, and was now UCC's registrar and registrar-designate of the new institution. It was he, above all, who charted a path for the executive commission through the swirling mass of problems great and small that confronted the new management of UCC, and ensured that the most important tasks were tackled first. It was also helpful that a joint working group had already produced draft charter and statutes. However, the proposed name for the new college, 'University of Wales, Cardiff', was vetoed by the University of Wales. In order not to lose momentum, a compromise had to be accepted, and what is now Cardiff University first saw the light under the cumbersome title of 'University of Wales College of Cardiff'. The commission's other main advantage was its power to take decisions swiftly and independently, by-passing the normal processes of consultation and consideration by committees. But tired and demoralized UCC staff could scarcely be expected to see this celerity as an advantage. The commission, though willing, found it difficult to keep the staff of both colleges as fully informed as both sides would have wished. Academic staff were unsure to what extent they could trust the incoming management to respect principles of collegiality in the new college. Meanwhile, managers wondered whether, when the authority of the executive commission had expired, much of their pioneering work might be undone by succeeding decision-making bodies. They need not have worried; the new senate and council seemed as determined as the executive commission had been to move forward positively, building on the progress made in that remarkable pre-merger year of 1987–8.

External validation of the commission's achievements came on 3 March 1989, when the full UGC paid a day-long visit to the new institution. Sir Peter Swinnerton-Dyer, the chairman, offered the committee's congratulations on what they had found. While stressing to the council the need to keep channels of communication with all levels of staff as open as possible, he said that the changes, the improvements and the extent to which true merger had been achieved were astonishing. In particular, the UGC were delighted that none of the students whom they had met had considered that merger had disrupted their studies. The success factors identified by Sir Peter – good luck and strong leadership – continue to be as relevant to all universities now as they were on that occasion in 1989.

The road to success

The university that emerged from the merger, though scarred, had immense potential, far greater than that of either of its parent institutions. First, its new principal, Sir Aubrey Trotman-Dickenson, had established a sound financial base, aided by the loan from the UGC. The university's outgoings, in particular its staff costs, had been reduced to levels compatible with its income by offers of early retirement and voluntary redundancy. The consolidation of academic departments had created larger and potentially more effective units. A considerable programme of relocations was an essential aspect of the merger. At its completion, the new departments were accommodated in good quality buildings, often refurbished, that were to prove adequate for the needs for some years to come. Engineering and physics benefited from the £30 million new complex, funded by one of the last major capital initiatives undertaken by the UGC.

In addition, the merger brought new management structures, developed by the principal in his previous role as head of UWIST. These were underpinned by a systematic resource allocation system, which replaced the obscure and arbitrary processes in UCC. The advantage of the new allocation system was not only that it provided simple administrative efficiency. It also transferred clear authority and consequently responsibility to heads of department. Heads of department were nominated by the principal after consultation with the department for endorsement by senate and appointment by council. This power enabled him to influence the character of departmental administration. Though by contemporary standards the administrative practices in the new institution appear unremarkable, there is no doubt that they were well in advance of the procedures then almost universally employed in comparable older universities. The platform that Sir Aubrey built was to prove more than adequate for the academic advances that were put in train later in the decade.

Finances at Cardiff were now on a secure footing and the estate was in good order; it was time to concentrate on developing the corporate culture, with a new emphasis on people. In 1993 a new vice-chancellor was appointed (by now the title of principal had been superseded). Brian Smith, who came from the mastership of an Oxford College, took as his brief Cardiff's extremely demanding (some would say foolhardy) objective, set shortly before his arrival, of becoming one of the UK's top 12 research-led universities. The challenge before him was to combine commitment to the highest possible academic standards with a more collegiate approach. Spirits began to lift as the university community embraced the new goal as top priority. The strategic focus now was on the recruitment and development of staff. A notable application of such a strategy, which served Cardiff as an exemplar, was the development of Stanford University in the period following the 1950s. This was initiated by the then provost Frederick Terman who, as a leading electrical engineer in the institution, had provided funds to help Bill Hewlett and David Packard launch the company that still bears their names. Terman was later credited 'almost wholly' with the developments that led to Silicon Valley (Allen 1980: 112). Terman's strategy was labelled 'steeples of excellence'. The steeples were selected key research areas led by the outstanding appointments he made. He realized, before others, that the appointment of world leaders in research was not necessarily expensive. Indeed, they often more than paid for themselves through their research grants and other external income, some of which accrued to the university through overhead charges. The energetic application of this strategy was to lead Stanford from its position as a sound but unremarkable US university to its current role as one of the world's leading centres of research and professional education. Cardiff was to employ a very similar strategy in its recovery from the crisis of the late 1980s.

Universities have many diverse responsibilities: the passing on of existing knowledge (teaching) and the discovery of new knowledge (research). In addition, they have a responsibility for cultural and economic development, particularly in their own region. These tasks can only be accomplished in an institution that creates an atmosphere in which staff and students alike can reach their full potential. In examining Cardiff's achievements it is convenient to look first at research. This is the most easily quantified of a university's outputs and it is also the activity that, perhaps for this reason, most determines a university's national and international standing.

In the first post-merger national review of research activity, the 1989 Research Assessment Exercise (RAE),[3] Cardiff was ranked at 38th, in the lower reaches of the 55 university institutions that existed at that time (and below both Aberystwyth and Swansea in Wales). The next RAE took place in 1992 and involved not only the established universities but also the new university institutions created from the polytechnics by the removal of the binary distinction. In this exercise Cardiff was placed 35th in the *THES* table of research excellence (*THES* 18 December 1992).

In the years that followed, great efforts were made to develop research at Cardiff. The principal feature was the focus on the recruitment and retention of leading academic researchers. The strategy was coordinated by a university-wide research committee, chaired by a pro vice-chancellor (for most of this period Professor Hadyn Ellis). Cardiff had been slow to set up such a committee, but when at last it did, it moved fast to utilize the abilities of its members. Each university department was allocated two mentors, one a member of the research committee and one the head of another (often cognate) department. Each department was expected to set up its own research committee to work with the head of department and the two mentors to develop and implement a departmental research strategy. The mentors spread best practice throughout the university and in doing so helped to minimize a competitive spirit, often not constructive, that had existed between departments prior to this initiative. This 'collegiality' produced throughout the institution a belief that the level of its overall success was the measure by which the university should be judged. The sense of a collective responsibility, which went beyond departments, did much to inculcate the corporate spirit that was to prove a major factor in the university's subsequent progress. The research committee drew its resources from a 10 per cent top-slice of the research funding granted to the university by the Higher Education Funding Council for Wales (HEFCW). These funds could be used to support initiatives that appeared particularly timely, and to provide seedcorn money to support the research of especially able young staff. Most attention was given to the provision of research support that would have relatively wide benefits, and especially to support that individual departments could not afford on their own.

At the same time the university embarked upon an active search for academic staff who were leading researchers. The recruitment was aided by an early retirement scheme, which, though valued by departments, presented them sometimes with difficult choices, since the scheme was funded by holding positions unfilled until the salary savings met the cost of the retirement. These offers of retirement were limited to cases where a clear benefit to the institution could be established. The number of staff who took advantage of this option was significant. For instance, in the academic year 1994–5 over 5 per cent of the established academic staff left under these arrangements and were replaced by research-active staff. In the two years 1994–5 to 1995–6, aided by the posts freed by early retirements, 164 new members of academic staff were recruited, of whom some 23 per cent were foreign nationals and a further 12 per cent were overseas residents. These new staff added significantly not only to the quality of the university's research activities, but also to the international atmosphere in which such work is best conducted.

Following the upheavals of the merger period, most people at Cardiff recognized that 'permanent change was here to stay' if the institution was to continue to advance. In this spirit, the university constantly reviewed the effectiveness of its departments. In the years from 1992 to 1996 one department was closed, with staff recruited by a neighbouring institution, and five others were merged in order to produce two new schools: molecular and medical biosciences, and engineering. These initiatives were the first of a continuing series of restructurings that enabled the university to evolve, and to refocus on new areas of research opportunity.

A chance to monitor the university's progress was provided by the 1996 RAE. The results were gratifying. In the *THES* table of research excellence (constructed on the same basis as the tables for 1989 and 1992, though the number of grades was increased), Cardiff was placed 15th out of 106 universities now assessed (*THES* 20 December 1996). Of the old civic universities, with which Cardiff might properly be compared, only Edinburgh and Bristol, at

13th and 14th place respectively, lay above Cardiff. This recognition of research excellence led to Cardiff's being invited to join the Russell Group of research-led universities two years later.

This signal achievement encouraged the university to continue with its strategies for vigorously promoting its research. The initiatives to recruit, offer early retirement and restructure departments continued. By 1999, thanks to closures and mergers, of the 29 departments existing in 1992 only 19 remained in their original form. Two new 'super-schools' were created. The school of social and administrative studies and the school of education were brought together to form a new school of social sciences, under the leadership of Professor Huw Beynon. Molecular and medical biosciences merged with pure and applied biology to form a school of biosciences headed by Professor Martin Evans, FRS, a pioneer of stem-cell research recruited from Cambridge. The impact of key new appointments was assessed by Professor Evans. He compared the research publications of the staff of the school of biosciences before and after some ten high-level new appointments were made when he took up the position of head of school. He found a very significant 11-fold increase in papers published in the field's three most prestigious journals. However, approximately half of this increase could be attributed to the higher performance of the staff who had been in the school prior to the reorganization and the new appointments. The value of key appointments was reflected not only by the new members' own contributions, but also by their capacity to bring out and enhance existing talents.

At the same time the administrative structure of the university was being adapted to meet the needs of the changing institution. A small management team, comprising pro vice-chancellors and senior executives, was set up. The flat structure in which departments dealt directly with the centre was enhanced when in 1998 faculties were abolished without raising any major concerns. The collaboration between departments had developed beyond traditional faculty boundaries and required new methods of support and encouragement. Since merger, departments had been funded directly from the centre, and the role of faculties had been somewhat marginal. The time saved by abolishing the associated committees represented a small but significant easing of the ever-increasing burdens on academic staff.

Following the obvious impact of the new recruits on research quality, as assessed by the 1996 RAE, the research committee embarked on a major new initiative. The sum of £4 million was accumulated from a variety of sources, and used to fund a new research fellowship programme. The scheme was unusually flexible.

Senior research fellows – distinguished professorial researchers – could be offered up to five years free from teaching and administrative responsibilities. Many, on recruitment, were offered the opportunity to join the established staff when the fellowship ended. Junior fellowships were for three years and again could lead to permanent positions if suitable posts were known to be becoming available at the appropriate time. The terms were found to be very attractive and, when the advertisement announcing the fellowships appeared, the personnel office found itself struggling to process more than 1200 applications. The quality of the applicants was judged to be higher than for traditional professorial or lectureship posts. More than 50 fellows were appointed, many from overseas.

The new research programmes were accompanied and indeed funded by a rapid growth in research grants gained (Figure 2.1). Research awards in 1992 were some £11 million; by 2001 they had

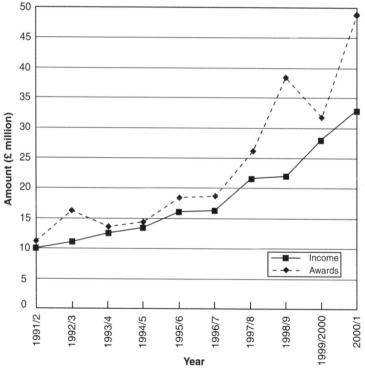

Figure 2.1   Cardiff University research awards and income, 1991–2001

reached nearly £50 million. A particular feature was the increase in research funding provided by the research councils, accounting for some 40 per cent (£20 million) of the total awards in 2001. This total included the first grant from the Leverhulme Trust to the Humanities to exceed £1 million: for the study of the impact of globalization on languages. There had been much concern in the early 1990s that Wales obtained only some 60 per cent of the support from research councils that might have been expected from its numbers of academic staff. This same low level was just as characteristic of Cardiff University as of Wales as a whole. However, the improvements since 1992, and particularly since 1996, showed that the university could reverse this deficit.

The year 2001 proved a good one to take stock and assess the university's progress. Dr David Grant CBE, previously director of technology at Marconi plc, took over as vice-chancellor, and the results of the 2001 RAE provided a measure of the current research activity. The table of research excellence published in the *THES* (14 December 2001) showed Cardiff to be seventh of the universities assessed, and highest placed of all the old civic universities. Only Oxford, Cambridge, the major London institutions and Warwick University were placed above it. (It is true that by now many different tables had been produced by the press, in some of which Cardiff showed less well, but the *THES* table, whose basis had been unchanged over the years, is the appropriate measure of the improved performance). The scale of the change can be illustrated by considering performances in more detail. In 1992 only some 30 per cent of Cardiff's units of assessment (essentially departments) were graded as 4 (national excellence) or better.[4] In 1996, 80 per cent and, in 2001, 95 per cent reached this level. In 1996, 45 per cent of Cardiff's units were rated at 5 (considerable international excellence) or above. By 2001, 86 per cent of units were 5 or 5+.

Research is the most easily assessed of a university's activities, and for this reason this account has devoted much attention to the quantifiable progress in that area. However, the primary duty of a university is teaching, and it is reassuring that Cardiff's progress in research has not been at the expense of teaching. Much effort has been made nationally to assess the quality of teaching as reliably as research has come to be evaluated. The Teaching Quality Assessment (TQA) attempts to rate departments or equivalent subject units as *excellent, satisfactory* and *unsatisfactory*, through systems of 'scoring' that have varied over the years and differ in England, Scotland and Wales. Furthermore, as the assessments are not made at a single time, it is extremely difficult, in evaluating the relative performance of institutions, to correct for the marked improvement in the average

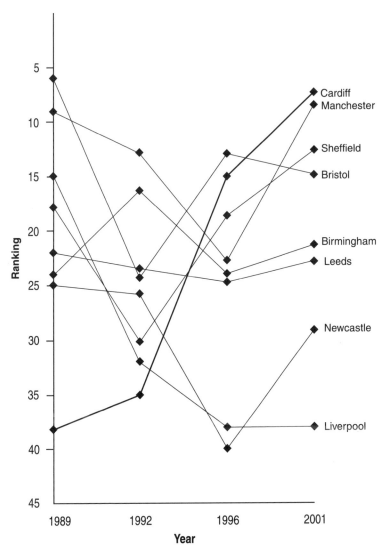

Figure 2.2   Ranking of selected universities in the Research
Assessment Exercises, 1989–2001

'scores' over time. But, with 50 per cent of its units rated *excellent* and
the rest *satisfactory*, Cardiff was placed 16th in the UK when
the assessments in Wales were completed in 1998 (*Daily Telegraph*
29 July 1998). (The early completion of the assessments in Wales and

a numerical scoring system introduced in England mean that the relative performance of Welsh universities will appear to deteriorate in the coming years.)

The university invested much effort into developing systems to ensure teaching quality. It created a teaching and learning committee, charged with establishing a policy to develop and improve teaching. At the same time, an academic quality assurance committee was set up to establish rigorous methods of confirming the quality of teaching within the institution through a process of regular departmental reviews conducted with external representatives on the reviewing panel. Cardiff's progress was confirmed in the report by the Quality Assurance Agency for Higher Education of its audit of March 2000. The report recognized the university's 'powerful academic vision' and commended its 'well-developed and effectively articulated mission to achieve excellence in teaching and research'.

The university also has important roles to play beyond its undergraduate and postgraduate teaching and its research. Cardiff has the largest programme of continuing education in Wales and its centres cover half the population of Wales. This activity survived the 1986–7 crisis unscathed. It has been continued and enhanced by the establishment of a centre for lifelong learning, dealing both with traditional continuing education and with the upgrading of professional skills. Each year about 8000 students enrol on its courses.

Since its establishment the university has been increasingly active in industrial liaison and in the support of local businesses, particularly small and medium-sized enterprises. In 1996 it founded the Cardiff University Innovation Network (CUIN) to encourage local companies to take advantage of the research expertise and extensive contacts that the university possesses. Regular meetings are held on a wide variety of topics chosen by an advisory board made up of the chairs and chief executives of local businesses. One rule that characterizes these meetings is that the number of academics, consultants and purveyors of professional services is not allowed to exceed the number of business representatives. The latter typically comprise 60 per cent of the attendees. The network was singled out for praise in the 2000 Science and Innovation White Paper (DTI 2000) as 'providing an effective bridge to facilitate technology transfer between academics, Welsh companies and business intermediaries'. CUIN prides itself on its practical 'hands-on' approach and has, directly or indirectly, found solutions to more than 750 problems brought to it by local businesses. One small firm from a South Wales valley, for example, found the answer to its problem in New York thanks to CUIN.

The expanding research base led to an increase in the intellectual property generated by the university. This was reflected in licensing income, which rose from £113,000 in 1998 to some £800,000 in 2001. The university, in conjunction with the University of Wales College of Medicine, was awarded £3 million from the University Challenge Seed Fund in 1999 to create the Cardiff Partnership Fund, to help to further develop intellectual property by increasing the numbers of spin-out companies created.

The initial development of the university following the crisis was largely carried out within the buildings available at the time of the merger in 1988. However, the success of the new institution, and especially the growth in its research activity, led to an ever-increasing demand for more space. By 1998, the university, which earlier in the decade had appeared to be so well provided for, had to seek to acquire additional sites and to build new accommodation for research and teaching. In 1999 the new school of social sciences, together with the department of city and regional planning, moved into the Glamorgan Building – a nearby civic building of some 7000 square metres, which had become available for purchase. In 2001, a new 400-seat lecture theatre, together with a computing resource centre, was completed. Further new buildings are under construction. A £12 million building for biosciences is nearing completion, while the Queen's Buildings in Newport Road are being extended in response to the ever-growing demands made by externally sponsored research. These developments will only partly meet demand, and the university is actively seeking to expand further.

All in all, the progress of Cardiff University since the crisis of the mid-1980s has been excellent – certainly much better than might have been predicted. It is interesting to speculate on the special factors that allowed Cardiff to change so dramatically when, on the whole, British universities have not found rapid change easy to achieve. The most obvious reason is the trauma of 1986–8. The university (or at least the UCC component) had been through a humiliating experience, made more difficult by the inability of UCC's decision-making bodies to force through the drastic steps necessary to avert disaster. This painful experience did much to banish the complacency often prevalent in statutory bodies such as universities. Cardiff's staff had experienced unpleasant change and were very prepared to accept the further changes that would lead to a financially stable and vigorous institution. In addition, clear and rigorous administrative practices were brought in at the time of the merger – practices that would have been more difficult to introduce in calmer times. The combination of these factors – a willingness to accept, even welcome, change, accompanied by the possibility of effective management by the central administration – provided great impetus. This was fuelled by the energy that resulted from the members of the institution experiencing the benefits brought by steady progress.

The above account may perhaps give the impression that progress at Cardiff was always smooth, rapid and unimpeded. But of course the university was confronted by the setbacks and disappointments that all institutions faced, including several departures of key members of staff. Much time had to be devoted by senior staff to the achievement of greater devolution within the University of Wales, while in 1996 tragedy struck in the form of a meningitis outbreak, during which two students died. Thus, the staff at Cardiff, both academic and non-academic, were in no way protected from the general experience elsewhere. An ever-increasing bureaucratic burden, founded to a large extent on ill-defined notions of account-ability, increasing student numbers not matched by increases in staff and salary awards that fell behind the norms for professional pay – all could have sapped staff morale. The fact that they failed to do so, and that the challenge of rebuilding Cardiff was met with energy and enthusiasm, speaks volumes for the character and determination of the university staff. It is to their great credit that the resurgence from the low point of the late 1980s to the success of the present time was achieved.

Conclusions

The inheritance of the pre-merger years is still discernible at Cardiff. Though the executive commission's powers of instant decision-making have been superseded by the more usual university processes of consultation and recommendation by subcommittee, there is still an expectation that, when necessary, action should be swift and decisive. So high was the level of trust in him that UCC's principal Bevan felt able to rule by decree, ignoring due process. Now, there is high awareness of the constitutional checks and balances that derive from the charter, and real appreciation of why they are there. The year 1987–8 saw revolutionary change, difficult for most staff, painful for many. In retrospect, the traumas of that year can be seen to have been hugely beneficial for the university as a whole, but it was not easy to re-engender trust in 'the centre' during the early post-merger years. The atmosphere then was more one of competition than of collaboration between departments. The successes of the 1990s have helped to shape a culture where academic departments help one another and trust 'the management' to lead the university forward to further achievements. The central planning function is particularly strong at Cardiff, and this, too, can be traced back to the days of the executive commission, when a series of successively more detailed plans for the future provided reassuring evidence to the outside world that Cardiff knew where it was going, and how it would get there.

The cost of the Cardiff crisis for individuals was undoubtedly high; many careers were disrupted and some were destroyed. Yet it led to the creation of a single, strong and successful institution, capable of taking its place among the leading UK universities. Thus, it could be argued that the crisis was ultimately to the advantage of higher education in Wales. The effects on British higher education as a whole are less easy to evaluate. Shattock (1994: 138) writes of the damage caused by 'the Cardiff affair' to the reputation of the UGC and to the university system as a whole. The great concern raised in the minds of the government about the manner in which universities were managed was certainly the most obvious result. The direct intervention of the UGC broke all the conventions that had been established to separate universities from government influence. From this time on government, often acting through the newly established funding councils, would play a much more interventionist role. It has been customary to regard this challenge to institutional autonomy as harmful to British higher education. Government control was thought to stifle initiative, crush diversity and make entrepreneurial risk-taking unacceptably dangerous; all these disadvantages were held to have arisen largely through UCC's irresponsibility. It is, however, possible to challenge this view. The government's wish to have a greater influence on the direction of higher education undoubtedly pre-dates the late 1980s. The Jarrett Committee brought out its recommendations on improving efficiency in universities in 1985, well before the difficulties at Cardiff became public knowledge. A convincing argument could be made that the Cardiff crisis played only a very small role in speeding the progress of the government's increasingly interventionist policies.

More controversially, it could be argued that the increasing interest of government in higher education may not have been wholly detrimental. In many ways, the closer link between government and universities has led to a period in which British higher education has been very successful. Undoubtedly the sector has faced ever-increasing bureaucracy, over-intrusive monitoring and an inability to pay appropriate salaries to its staff, which must threaten its future capability. But during the 1990s universities managed the greatest expansion in their history with only a modest increase in staff. There is considerable evidence that the sector's research outputs have improved in both quality and quantity, as seen not only in the increase in worldwide citations, but also in the growth and development of intellectual property through licensing agreements and spin-out companies.

Certainly the consequences of the Cardiff crisis may be far from negative. But perhaps this is a matter that can best be decided by those in the future who will view these dramatic events from the comfort of greater distance.

Appendix: The Research Assessment Exercise

The Research Assessment Exercise (RAE) provides ratings of research quality in virtually all academic disciplines (called units of assessment). In 1996 and 2001, a scale based on the grades 1, 2, 3a, 3b, 4, 5 and 5* was used. The grades are defined:

5* Attainable international excellence in more than half of research areas and attainable levels of national excellence in the remainder.
5   Attainable levels of international excellence in up to half of the research areas and attainable levels of national excellence in virtually all of the remainder.
4   Attainable levels of national excellence in virtually all research areas, with some evidence of international excellence.
3a Attainable levels of national excellence in more than two-thirds of research areas, possibly showing evidence of international excellence.
3b Attainable levels of national excellence in more than half of the research areas.
2   Attainable levels of national excellence in up to half of the research areas.
1   Attainable levels of national excellence in none, or virtually none, of the areas of research activity.

The table of research excellence for universities derived by *The Times Higher Education Supplement* averages the grades, by associating them with a seven-point numerical scale, weighted by the staff numbers submitted in each unit of assessment. In 1989 and 1992, a five-point scale was used, averaged in the same manner. Since 1996, alternative ranking tables have been introduced. One used in *The Times* averages the grades over *all* staff, not just those submitted. Thus, whereas the *THES*'s table ranks the *quality* of research output, *The Times*'s table emphasizes the 'research environment', in that the presence of non-research-active staff lowers the performance. The journal *Research Fortnight* uses a scale of what it terms 'research power': the *THES*'s average grade multiplied by the number of staff submitted. Thus, research power also takes into account the *quantity* of research undertaken in an institution.

To enable us to refer back to 1989, we have used the *THES* table as the basis of our comparisons.

Acknowledgements

The authors wish to express their gratitude to the authorities at Cardiff University for their ready help in the preparation of this chapter, and especially for the generous and unstinting assistance of Louise Casella, Eirian Edwards, Geraint Jones and Mike Joynson. They also gladly acknowledge a debt of thanks to Dr Gethin Williams, who allowed them to consult a draft of the initial chapters of his forthcoming study *The University College Cardiff Crisis of 1986–87 Revisited – Origins and Outcomes*. When published, this should provide the most comprehensive account of the events outlined in this chapter. Although Vanessa Cunningham is the main author of the first half of this chapter and Brian Smith of the second, we take joint responsibility for the entire chapter.

Notes

1 Shattock, then registrar of the University of Warwick, headed the team of professionals who were sent into UCC by the UGC in the spring of 1987 to assess the college's financial position and recommend remedies.
2 Letter from UGC chairman, quoted in Executive Commission minute no. 179.1.
3 In this exercise, academic units (usually but not always academic departments) were given a numercial score (see Appendix). The average scores, weighted by the number of staff in each unit of assessment, determine the published ranking lists. This system was universally adopted until 1997, when a variety of different ways of producing national rankings were introduced.
4 See the Appendix for a full explanation of RAE scales.

3

CAPITAL BUILDING AND CASH FLOW AT THE UNIVERSITY OF LANCASTER

Marion McClintock and William Ritchie

This chapter gives a condensed account of an acute financial crisis at Lancaster, at its height between 1995 and 1997, and shows how external pressures for development, especially in relation to the capital building programme, and internal historical factors combined to threaten the future of an academically strong institution. The resolution of the crisis provides examples of the need to combine rigorous financial planning with wider academic and managerial changes.

Lancaster: the first 25 years

Lancaster was the seventh and last of the new greenfield universities that were founded in the early 1960s. Like its contemporaries, it had come about as the result of a bid by the local authority, in this case Lancashire County Council. The city had already been identified as being one of several regional centres, well removed from existing universities, with good accessibility to its region, a substantial population hinterland, good accommodation facilities and promising cultural facilities (Balchin 1959). It was, however, not until 23 November 1961 that the case for Lancaster had been accepted. The first students were admitted less than three years later, when 330 undergraduates and postgraduates assembled in the former Waring and Gillows premises in central Lancaster, to be taught by the first 50 or so staff recruited across the range of core subjects.

Much was asked of these new institutions. Most civic universities had served long apprenticeships as university colleges. Keele in the late 1940s had, however, moved more quickly to full university status, and by the time Sussex was being planned the device of an academic planning board, backed up by an academic advisory committee, to monitor the new institution had led in 1961 to the immediate award of charter and statutes and the autonomy they gave. This example set a precedent for the other new foundations, including Lancaster, for whom the Queen in Council approved both charter and statutes on 14 September 1964. As a consequence of these apparent privileges, the new institutions were compelled to perform on a comparable basis with foundations much more securely established in terms of subject coverage, teaching quality and research output. Lancaster was therefore put under strain from the outset; enhanced in this case by the relative isolation of north Lancashire, necessitating the university being self-sufficient in all the facilities that it needed. This self-sufficiency was reflected particularly in the capital building programme, where an area of open parkland between the A6 and M6 highways was transformed into a working institution in five years (1964–9).

Teaching space was funded by the UGC, although space and quality norms were being reduced during the 1960s, and UGC funding of residential space in the first two colleges, Bowland and Lonsdale, was also provided. Thereafter the university was on its own: the County College's student accommodation was the result of a £0.5 million gift from Lancashire, while Cartmel, Furness and Fylde relied on commercially sponsored student blocks, a scheme initiated by Charles Carter (McClintock 1974: 74). Specialist facilities also had to be funded from the university's own resources, and a University Appeal Fund, led by the Earl of Derby, raised £2.57 million by February 1971. This was wisely and well spent on essential expenditure, including residential and staff accommodation, cultural and welfare facilities, contributions to academic posts, supplementing Treasury shortfalls (including the telephone exchange and basic computer equipment), indoor and outdoor recreational facilities, commercial facilities for the university and a small fund for the embellishment of the university (McClintock 1974: 419). Nevertheless, a sum of an order of magnitude greater was probably needed.

The objective for Lancaster was to reach a student population of 3000 within ten years, and this was duly accomplished. The second generation of subjects was developed, primarily in the social sciences (McClintock 1994: 6): no new major disciplines have been added since the introduction of law in 1978, although the diversity of schemes of study has not been correspondingly inhibited.

In 1981, however, the chairman of the UGC declared there would be a significant loss of income for 1983–4 across the university system. While Lancaster's reduction in recurrent grant was of an average size of 15 per cent, the consequences included the loss of several areas of language (including Russian, a foundation subject), a decline in student numbers, a process of voluntary severance and a temporary cessation of the capital building programme. This initial crisis proved to be a foretaste of what was to come, and undoubtedly helped to store up problems for the future. One positive aspect of the period, however, was that as the university moved back into modest surplus, the vice-chancellor of the time, Professor Philip Reynolds, and the development committee agreed to release funds for research and invited bids area by area for the sums available. This decision critically boosted the development of a research-led culture that had been slow to become established in the busy opening years and the period of financial difficulty. Part of the report from a UGC visit in May 1985 was a comment on how far ahead of other institutions Lancaster was in taking this initiative.

The third vice-chancellor, Professor Harry Hanham, took up his post in 1985, with far-reaching objectives and a decade in which to fulfil them. They included a substantial increase in the student population and associated staffing, a rise in the profile of the university, regionally, nationally and internationally, and a determination that Lancaster would become a teaching and research university. The outcome of the first Research Assessment Exercise, in 1986, placing Lancaster midway in the first of many league tables, strengthened his resolve to highlight research as a priority. The 1989 exercise showed Lancaster as 16th nationally, while in the 1992 exercise it appeared in the top ten of universities for the first time. This level of research quality, once established, has been maintained in the subsequent RAE outcomes by remaining in similar positions in 1996 and 2001.

In this decade, student numbers doubled, and there was increasing emphasis on postgraduate taught courses, especially in the management school. Links with two associate colleges, Blackpool and The Fylde, and Blackburn, were added to the external validating relationships with Edge Hill College and St Martin's College, which had been in place with the university for more than two decades. There was a determination to reorganize – faculties were tentatively established from 1987 onwards – and a substantial programme of capital expenditure began.

The nature of the crisis

The fundamental nature of Lancaster's problem was twofold: a lack of resources and other liquid assets, and excessive pressure on the cash flow of the university, leading to the institution being unable to sustain its programme of development. The main pressure point was the capital expenditure programme, but the short-lived move into and out of direct participation in initial teacher training also played an important part.

The university had found itself with a difficult dilemma at the beginning of the 1990s, with a need simultaneously to expand its student numbers, especially at the postgraduate level, to develop its research capability, to renew and replace its academic staff by recruits from a new generation and to meet the challenges of international, national and regional roles. The choice, in the view of the vice-chancellor of the day, was either to break through into competition with peer institutions throughout the UK or to ossify as a pleasant but rather isolated backwater. Each constraint had an impact on the next: for example, the lack of teaching and appropriate residential accommodation hampered the intake of significantly larger student numbers; equally, the absence of a large critical mass of students of all types, including part-timers, limited the generation of the necessary funds to make capital funding available. The university had taken full advantage of the earlier business expansion schemes to develop more residential space. These schemes were, however, no longer available when the next phase of expansion became necessary, and in any case there was an immediate need for additional teaching and library space that did not generate immediate revenue returns. Student dissatisfaction was rising: after a rent strike and sit-in in October 1991 student leaders not only cited rental levels as being unreasonably high, but pointed to growing dissatisfaction at the condition of some residential areas, and their lack of refurbishment.

A paper of May 1994 to the senate by the then vice-chancellor, written as preparation for the estates strategy required by the HEFCE, remains the best analysis of the problems relating to the capital pro-gramme. It placed at centre stage the Bain report on private sector funding in higher education, which had received the imprimatur of all four funding councils. It encouraged institutions to contemplate setting up long-term relationships with financial institutions, either through a consortium of institutions sharing a bond issue or by a capitalized vehicle company that would 'act as a conduit for finance from the capital market' (Bain 1993: 28) on behalf of such a con-sortium, by generating loans that would be multiples of the initial investment by consortium members. It was, however, stressed that the vehicle company 'would be a creature of the private sector. There would be no involvement by the Funding Councils in actively setting it up or in managing it afterwards.'

In the meantime, Lancaster had been awarded £1.39 million of a

£10 million HEFCE initiative for an extension of the library, on condition that the university raised the balance of over £4 million. A
deterioration in the quality of the local student housing market
meant that the university felt the need to provide more rooms at
Bailrigg: up to 500 in October 1995 at an estimated cost of £7 million
were planned, with another 500 a year later, by a development of
part of the open south-west corner of the university's land. A plan
for rehousing the students' union with new offices and upgraded
shopping facilities, which had been under discussion for several years,
was now ready for implementation, at an estimated cost of £2.4
million. While the newly completed George Fox Building had
generated essential additional lecture theatres, and the management
school graduate school some attractive teaching space, there was a
growing backlog of office space at the southern end of the university.
The existing teaching laboratories were too large and obsolete, and
hence underused: their replacement by smaller, better equipped and
more fully utilized laboratories was becoming an urgent priority.
There was also a need for more research laboratory space, especially
for the second wave of science subjects: computing, engineering and
psychology.

The vice-chancellor reported within a paper of June 1994 that
the Council had appointed Barclays de Zoete Wedd as consultants.
They would first be asked to rationalize an existing complex loan
portfolio of amounts ranging between £200,000 and over £3 million,
and totalling £13 million. Second, they would be asked to obtain
additional external capital of around £33 million, which with the
£13 million would meet the £50 million that Bain had concluded
would be the minimum economic threshold for an individual bond.

Over the next 11 months, therefore, with many twists and turns on
the way, Lancaster became the first university to have a listed security
on the London Stock Exchange: an issue of £35 million of 9.75 per
cent First Mortgage Debenture Stock 2025 on 5 April 1995. The interest, at a rate well above the subsequent prevailing interest rates, was to
be paid quarterly; the university would redeem the stock at the end of
the 30-year period, and meanwhile would build up a redemption
fund. The capital security of properties owned by the university for
the stock was £66 million, i.e. 1.89 times the notional value of the
bond. The proceeds were to be used to repay existing debts, with the
balance to be added temporarily to the resources of the university,
pending investment in property. The expenses relating to the transac-
tion totalled almost exactly £1 million, and the university now had to
meet the exacting demands of a trustee and of the London Stock
Exchange.

The university was also carrying the following forward capital commitments relating to BES schemes that were coming to fruition: £6.52 million from BES for residences not earlier than October 1995, and not later than October 1998 at a higher level of £7.387 million; Lancaster University Residences I and II between March and May 1998 at a cost of £2.748 million and £5.9 million respectively; and Lancaster University Residences III on 13 September 1998 at a cost of £4.2 million. Partial loan facilities, arranged in advance from the Royal Bank of Scotland, were to be on hand to facilitate these arrangements.

Another significant diversion of time, energy and money related to the merger of Charlotte Mason College at Ambleside in Cumbria with the university in 1992. The college, whose main activity was initial teacher training, had been an associated institution of Lancaster since 1967. Although in 1989 it had been incorporated as an independent higher education institution, in the same year steps towards a full merger with the university were initiated, on grounds of its size, scale and vulnerability. A working party of the senate had been set up in March 1992 to consider the academic aspects of the merger, while the financial affairs were the responsibility of a council working party (Rowe 1997: 80).[1]

While the merger seemed to fulfil the logic of the long association between the two institutions, and the aspirations of the university for an enhancement of its regional role, in practice the university was acquiring an additional liability. First, no independent appraisal of the college's academic quality was carried out, and the longer-term consequences of an adverse report dating from January 1992 by Her Majesty's Inspectors about the work of the college became the responsibility of a university with no previous experience of initial teacher training. Second, despite the history and the natural grandeur of the college's location, investment in its infrastructure was urgently needed to bring the college up to the standards required by OFSTED, especially a new library. Third, the university was taking on staff with different terms and conditions of service from its own staff, and with different expectations about their own future development. The university, perhaps for the first time, had acquired an activity that was sufficiently distant from its core functions to pose a threat to its future reputation and financial viability (see also below).

There were of course other problems. The student numbers allocated for Lancaster by the HEFCE were first expanded and then consolidated, and expectations of further growth were not fulfilled. The university had aspired to become research-led, especially when it had appeared in the top ten for the first time in 1992. The steps necessary to sustain this achievement, including the appointment of staff with strong research profiles, the replacement and upgrading of equipment and laboratory facilities and the continuation of the generous but critically important sabbatical leave provision, all put pressure on a university that would always be operating at the outer limit of its resources.. When the various pressures interacted with each other, as they were to do in 1995–6 and 1996–7, the situation for the university became very grave.

In addition, late in 1993 the council set up a joint search committee for a successor to Professor Hanham, who was due to retire in September 1995. A new vice-chancellor, Professor William Ritchie, was duly appointed to take up office in October 1995. He, like other members of the university, was unaware of the deep financial problems that lay ahead.

How were the problems discovered?

The discovery and analysis of the university's problems fell into two phases. The first was during 1995–6, when the council and its senior committees sought to understand the problem that had emerged with such remarkable rapidity and cope with it. A second and more public phase began in the summer of 1996. An investigation, commissioned from the university's external auditors in September 1995, began the process of discovery; the university's audit committee was clear and explicit in making known to the council the main heads of disquiet; the council acted appropriately in response to the information supplied; and the HEFCE was kept fully informed. During the second phase, more emphasis fell on the attitude of the university's bankers, and the measures to be taken involved the senate as well as the council. As the difficulties mounted, however, the appropriate control mechanisms continued to function, and were fully supported by senior officers. A brief account of the escalating difficulties is necessary in order to understand the remedial action subsequently taken.

In May 1995 the council approved in principle a new residential development on its hitherto undeveloped South-West Campus, and approved the library extension. In July 1995 the contract for the building of the Ruskin Library, funded principally by the Heritage Lottery Fund, was given approval. The Tower Avenue development was under construction, and an extensive programme of minor works was planned, giving a total capital expenditure programme of £20 million, the bulk of it in 1995–6. During the summer, however, as the cash position deteriorated, the outgoing vice-chancellor commissioned a special report from the external auditors, KPMG, which was received by the new vice-chancellor late in October and the audit committee in November. As a consequence, in December 1995 the council was told that revised income and expenditure forecasts for 1995–6 showed a deficit of £2.15 million, and that the ambitious capital programme, with low contingency allowances, was showing signs of exceeding budgeted expenditure and was exerting considerable pressure on cash flow. The unsecured borrowing of the university had already exceeded £3 million once, which was in excess of the £2 million limit in the financial memorandum from the HEFCE. It would do so again in July 1996, and the projections for the end of the planning period, in 1998–9, showed the same degree of strain. In addition, a premature retirement scheme was not being adequately controlled.

The HEFCE began much closer monitoring of Lancaster's financial affairs, including the receipt of quarterly financial reports from November 1995 onwards. Although there was a moment in March 1996 when the projected overdraft for the end of 1998–9 was calculated to be over £7 million, a resolution of the position was reached without KPMG having to qualify the already approved 1994–5 annual accounts. There was indeed some optimism by May 1996 that problems had been faced, that the HEFCE would give approval to a bank loan facility of £4.8 million and that a proposed sale and leaseback of the South-West Campus development might ease the pressures on cash flow. An action plan was agreed and aspects of it were being implemented during the 1995–6 academic year (see the next section).

On 5 July 1996 the council was, however, unable to agree the budget for 1996–7 as presented to it, and the university secretary, while reporting that a short-term borrowing facility of £4.8 million had been agreed with NatWest and the HEFCE for the period to 31 July 1996, also told the council that further borrowing, to a sum unspecified, would be required until mid-October. By the time the council reassembled on 24 July, following a meeting of the finance and general purposes committee earlier the same day, members were told that a request had been made to the HEFCE for short-term borrowing of up to £9.5 million for the two months of August and September 1996. By now NatWest was requiring more detailed analysis of the university's request for a secured loan of up to £7 million, in addition to an unsecured loan of £2 million or more; and the day after the council had met, the local manager wrote to Coopers and Lybrand, seeking a financial and structural analysis of the university's position. This firm of accountants had a branch specializing in higher education, and was often called in when institutions were facing severe financial difficulty. In the meantime, the disposal of the South-West Campus, proposed in order to reinject cash into the university, had run into significant logistical and legal difficulties. The proposal was subsequently terminated.

The summer of 1996 was a distressing period for Lancaster since, as the pro-chancellor reported to the council that October:

> Early in August . . . the bank told the University it was not willing to underpin all of its needs for short- and medium-term finance unless the institution committed itself to a radical recovery plan that would clear the core overdraft problem by 1999–2000: a similar message also came from the HEFC(E). A letter had been sent to Council members in early September . . . [Senior officers] had prepared a set of proposals for presentation to the crucial meeting with the bankers and the HEFC(E) on 26 September.[2]

Other, less formal, meetings also took place, including an un-scheduled evening gathering in August. As the court was reminded retrospectively by the vice-chancellor in February 2002:

> To be dramatic, Lancaster had been one of the first to taste the hemlock, the bitter realism personified in the senior bankers, bondholders and men in grey suits who had told [senior officers] the facts of life one evening six years ago . . . [They] had been told they would get no help from the Funding Council, nor financial institutions, nor bondholders, but rather that the University was autonomous and should make its own way.[3]

In addition to addressing the growing financial crisis, wider man-agerial issues had to be considered. Before Christmas 1995 the new vice-chancellor had met with the chairman of the HEFCE to describe the serious financial situation in the university, and the two remained in contact. As expected, when the full extent of the difficulties became apparent in the summer of 1996, the HEFCE was unwilling to do other than reschedule monthly payments of the recurrent grant and to pay for 50 per cent of the costs of the Coopers and Lybrand review.

As an interim measure, tight financial controls were placed on all activities, no further capital expenditure was allowed and steps were taken to determine the possibility of selling some of the few assets which were available to the university. The crisis management team VCSAG (vice-chancellor's strategic advisory group) was set up and worked on a project basis, in order to tackle the separate but interrelated pressing financial and related problems. Although the problem was inherently financial, VCSAG concluded that an equally important management issue was to maintain the morale of the academic and other staff who were astonished and angry at the precipitous decline in the financial stability of the university and the consequent impact on their day-to-day activities. These managerial difficulties were even more acute at Charlotte Mason College, especially once the discussions with St Martin's College became public knowledge (see below). The only remedy in both institutions was for the vice-chancellor to hold open discussions, attend mass meetings, make departmental visits and give clear position statements to every meeting of senate and council. Put simply, the financial crisis could not be allowed to undermine the confidence of all staff who were working in a research-led university of international reputation. Restoring confidence was also vital to staff retention, and hence small inputs were made to new initiatives, although many had to be postponed with a promise of assistance when recovery was achieved. The compromise solution of retreating into a pre-dominantly teaching university, at the expense of top-class research with associated support facilities, was rejected from the outset. Although considered briefly, some type of merger with any other university was also discarded.

What was done to correct the problems

Although a recovery plan was agreed by the council in December 1996, many of the measures it included were already in hand by then. It is also important to recognize that, even at the height of the crisis, the university's academic activities of teaching, learning, assessment and research continued unabated, and when the results of the 1996 RAE were published in December, Lancaster again appeared in the top ten of national league tables.

At this point it is appropriate to return to Charlotte Mason College. After the integration of the college into the university in 1992 (see above), the work of its departments had been organized in a variety of different ways, including through a faculty of teacher education and training from 1994. The new structure was, however, somewhat remote both physically and conceptually from the day-to-day work of the college. An adverse OFSTED report late in 1995 of the training in English and mathematics resulted in four ratings each of unsatisfactory and revealing deficiencies, which, on a preliminary estimate, could only be solved by making significant staff and structural changes, which in turn would require substantial financial input. Direct discussions were held with the chairperson of OFSTED, who, while sympathetic, could offer no direct assistance. As the CRILL report noted:

The immediate effect of this was to reduce the allocation of numbers, remove the opportunity for special bids, and render teacher training liable to further inspection ... remedial action needed to be swift, as further failure would result in the removal of accreditation.

(Rowe 1997: 161)

Fortunately, St Martin's College, situated at Bowerham in Lancaster, already enjoyed a strong track record with the TTA in initial teacher training, and its principal, after being approached by the vice-chancellor, made an offer to take Charlotte Mason under St Martin's wing. Negotiations took place during 1996 with the TTA and the HEFCE, as well as with St Martin's, about the terms on which such a transfer might take place. A project group, reporting to the vice-chancellor, undertook an options appraisal, and the option to allow St Martin's to take over teacher training proved the most likely to safeguard the academic futures of staff and students and to be the most cost-effective. In practice, the university had to bear the cost of an early retirement and voluntary severance scheme prior to transfer, and lost £1 million per annum in overheads of fees, TTA subvention and general revenue earned from the 1000 students involved. While the move proved to be correct for Charlotte Mason and the university in the medium term, in the short term the transfer added significantly to the pressures on the university's financial and management overload.

The primary approach for recovery was to be a draconian, progressive, but not fatally damaging reduction of cost in every area of the university. Inevitably the single largest item was staff costs, where voluntary severance and early retirement were supported by a certain amount of unpaid leave of absence but more by vacant posts being left empty as long as possible. A precise analysis of the reduction is made difficult because of the earlier plans by the university, before the financial difficulties became apparent, to remodel the age profile of staff, and hence to encourage a steady flow of early departures. During the budgeting period of spring 1996, however, a new scheme had released a tide of early retirements. Two hundred and ten volunteers elected to leave the university, although the proportions were skewed more towards voluntary severance than expected, and to assistant rather than academic staff. The consequences were uneven in terms of the areas where the departures were most commonplace, and buy-back arrangements for a considerable proportion of the academic staff who left, in order to cover necessary teaching, were commonplace. Although there were recriminations about lack of control of the May 1996 exercise, and some overrun of budget, the exercise led to substantial reductions in staff costs for the purposes of the recovery plan, and a later date of commencement would, with hindsight, have been deleterious.

Some lay members of the council pushed strongly for the setting up of a redundancy committee, but this move was resisted at all levels and, although not forgotten, was not implemented. Instead a special working group of the council under the chairmanship of the deputy vice-chancellor examined every conceivable type of payroll reduction, only to discover that many were impracticable or legally dubious, such as the non-implementation of an agreed pay award. Nor were all posts frozen: while the numbers of approvals slowed to a small trickle, key areas of the university could still make a case through the vice-chancellor to a small but central appointing group. Another helpful device, the concept of building significant gap savings into the budget, was imported to Lancaster by the new vice-chancellor. This process involved the deferral of filling even such posts as were approved as long as possible, a procedure that proved so effective it has become a routine feature of the university's annual budget-setting processes. A commitment was given not to expect relatively vulnerable groups, such as staff on fixed-term contracts, to show disproportionate savings. This category of staff was however pencilled in for a saving of £2.3 million over the period, from a total staff savings target of £23 million over four years. Staff costs were projected to fall by almost £10 million per annum between 1995–6 and 1997–8. Although the actual net reduction was just over half this amount, the lessening of salary-related pressures, even if short-lived, made a considerable impact on the underlying cash flow problem and, especially important, signalled a willingness to take and to implement uncomfortable decisions.

In terms of external assistance, the bank was prepared, on the basis of two- or three-month periods at a time during the autumn of 1996, to advance the necessary fluctuating overdrafts, and the HEFCE to authorize them on a short-term basis, at the cost of close monitoring. The intervention and close relationship of Coopers and Lybrand through the summer and autumn of 1996 to the recovery process in turn provided a verification to external bodies that the measures the university was taking were correct, sufficient and effective.

The next obvious area for reduction was capital expenditure and exposure. First, assets were as far as possible disposed of, the most notable being the 150-acre Hazelrigg site, situated on the other side of the M6 motorway from the university, which had been purchased by auction in 1965. The university sought to draw back from use of premises in Lancaster's city centre, at the Storey Institute, and to sell peripheral houses and land at Bailrigg. The capital building programme was in effect suspended, other than the completion of projects for which commitments had already been made. Major maintenance, despite the misgivings of the audit committee, was scaled back to the level that satisfied statutory health and safety requirements, and minor works were cut to £250,000 a year. The equipment allocation, which had reached a budgeted level of £2 million for 1995–6, was for 1996–7 first cut to £600,000 and then further to £200,000. Even the purchase of furniture for the new library extension was deferred.

While the council discussed staffing and capital expenditure, the senate was preoccupied by an academic action plan that was intended to involve the removal of specified activities or even whole departments, and certainly to achieve a significant and lasting net reduction in the number of staff. While initially radical, the plans were tempered in the light of discussion to more moderate realignments that none the less gave a more assured basis for identifying where such appointments as could be made were most urgent.

During this period of planning for financial recovery, it was recognized that some of the underlying difficulties related to the university's governance and management. While these issues were not made as explicit, the vice-chancellor advised both the council and the senate that over a period these areas would be reviewed and restructured, in order to increase efficiency and managerial effectiveness. Thus a review of committees and working groups, already initiated by the deputy vice-chancellor, was intensified in order to reduce the number of committees, the frequency of their meetings and the size of their membership. The number of faculties was reduced from seven to five, and there was a consolidation of their structure, including clearer guidelines for the role of the deans in the management structure, with increased oversight and control by them of departmental budgets.

The VCSAG was quickly converted to a strategic and tactical university management advisory group, composed of senior academic and administrative managers, but with the term advisory left in the title to signal the ultimate subservience in governance terms to the office of the vice-chancellor, and to the council and the senate. Other parts of the overall management structure were left intact for the time being in key support areas, such as the library and information systems services. There was also a conscious decision to resist external and internal pressures to alter departmental academic and managerial structures early in the recovery plan period.

The administration was required to carry a significant proportion of cuts, and was restructured into two divisions. The first was the academic division, headed by the university secretary, which included registry and student support functions, validation and monitoring of academic provision and the regulatory framework, governance and oversight of the committee structure, and recruitment and marketing. The second was the resources division, including finance, personnel, estates, strategic purchasing, security and portering, services to colleges and trading operations.

No area of the university was exempt from cost cutting and reduction of activity. There was a moratorium on non-essential expenditure, and for a while even minor purchases had to be approved at the level of the faculty dean. Actions included stopping subscriptions to international bodies and prohibiting promotional or other overseas travel by the vice-chancellor and senior officers, other than for international student recruitment, eliminating almost all expenditure on institutional entertainment or social functions and making no physical improvement to accommodation in University House. These actions were considered to be of great importance in fostering a belief that everything possible was being done to save money; a sense of frugality which had a resonance with the Quaker origins of the university under its first vice-chancellor. Even if some savings were minor, the sense that every member of the university was involved in solving the problem was appreciated by the whole university community – which as a campus- and college-based university has an acute and village-like awareness of the institution's closest workings. In that context, the decision by the vice-chancellor in July 1996 to set up a small review group to consider institutional lessons to be learned (the CRILL report) was in keeping with the ethos of openness that is characteristic of Lancaster. The report, published a year later to the council and the senate, remains a frequently quoted document.

Thus credible financial planning, managerial restructuring and the incorporation of a value-for-money approach into all university transactions were essential components of the recovery plan. More qualitative, intangible and undocumented factors also played a critical part in the rapid recovery of the institution, including a message from the top of the university that there was no fatal crisis but a rational expectation of recovery within a few years, coupled with the confidence that the core business of teaching and research continued to be robust and of national and international standing.

While it would be wrong to gloss over the sense of dislocation and even panic felt by many staff, most accepted the need for change. Some naturally found it difficult to accept the position that the university would become finance-led and business-like in the execution of its core activities, and saw a threat of relative decline in collegiality and in academic-led decision-making. In the event most of these fears were unfounded and, to a certain extent, Lancaster anticipated the financial and managerial challenges to the UK higher education sector of the 1990s.

The recovery plan period was for 48 months, from 1 August 1996 to 31 July 2000, with the aim that the projected deficit of £9 million at 31 July 1997 should be eliminated by the end of the period, and that an annual 5 per cent surplus on turnover should be achieved thereafter, in order to lay the foundations for essential future investment. In the meantime the university had to rely on close co-operation between its external auditors and the appropriate bodies of the university, to avoid having the university's accounts qualified, or the university being categorized as not a going concern, particularly in respect of the 1995–6 accounts as they worked their way through the approvals process at the end of 1996 and the first weeks of 1997. Equally, the process of setting the budget for 1997–8, by a director of finance newly in post, was especially demanding, requiring steady nerves in those with the most intimate knowledge of the university's finances. Nevertheless, the university performed well ahead of target in each successive financial year of the recovery plan period and achieved the 5 per cent surplus in three successive years (1998, 1999 and 2000), while at the same time continuing to build up staff numbers, receive excellent subject review reports and make preparations for RAE 2001.

The process of change and restructuring continued throughout the period. An important two-day conference with members of senate and council took place in May 1998 in order to map out strategic options, including the setting of major research priorities based on proven interdisciplinary strengths. Another critical step in the process of rebuilding was the successful application to the HEFCE earlier in the same year for special investment funding of £1.865 million over three years in the two strategic growth areas of environment and communications systems, which in turn led to growth for the future (see next section). Further changes in the structure of the senior academic management were made, a process completed in 2001 when four pro vice-chancellors were in post with the following responsibilities: academic development; research and resources; college, staff and student affairs; third mission funding from the EU and regional agencies. In addition, two directors for undergraduate and postgraduate studies were appointed, while the post of dean for the university's associated institutions highlighted the importance of these relationships as part of Lancaster's crucial regional role within the North West of England. There was also an increase in emphasis on sketching out plans for new investment and future growth, including a comprehensive corporate plan and estates strategy and more explicit targets for such areas as student recruitment, including from overseas.

The system of financial control was made more seamless, with a budget-setting process that flowed out of a mid-year review, and close monitoring of expenditure by a budget review group chaired by the vice-chancellor. While major efforts for additional income generation were to come by design later in the recovery period, steps were taken to enhance the flow of donations from the university's alumni and a profit-related pay scheme was also modestly helpful in contributing to the university's infrastructure in the library and information systems services.

A particularly crucial step, in the period 1997–9, was the consolidation of the university's long-term debt profile. This process included a restructuring of the £35 million debenture stock so that the university now deals with a single counter-party instead of an unlimited number of stockholders, has a debt service fund that enables the capital outstanding to be reduced year by year and has eliminated the potential for additional property to be tied up as security for the loan. The credit rating of A– by Standard and Poor early in 2002 is further evidence of how the attitudes and structures developed in the aftermath of the crisis have had the effect of placing Lancaster in a strong position to meet the challenges of future years.

The future

Forecasts of the future are almost certainly doomed to fail, but the certainty for Lancaster is that its tight financial discipline will continue and it will have to continue to strive energetically for its successes. There will be no easy answers for the university or its members in the years ahead.

None the less, the immediate position has been transformed within the five years since the crisis was at its height. The 2001 RAE confirmed for the third time the excellence of Lancaster's overall research profile, and grants from the European Regional Development Fund will be put to excellent use by the university. The capital programme, after a prolonged pause during the recovery plan period, is again accelerating. The 1998 investment in the area of environmental and biological sciences helped in early negotiations with the NERC that led to the setting up of the Lancaster Environment Centre and the impending transfer in 2003 of ITE Merlewood to a new building on the university campus. Similarly, Computing and Communications Systems are expected to move into new purpose-built accommodation, InfoLab 21, in 2004, alongside third mission commercial activities related to technology transfer in the North West. In both cases, the lesson was applied that secure external funding must be in place in advance of letting a contract, and business plans approved for the running costs of the new activities. The university is also about to embark on a major building programme of additional or replacement student accommodation, the difference being that from the outset there will be an external partner and the whole programme will be conducted off balance sheet. Because of the burgeoning market for overseas students, and the demands of parents who are paying their student children's fees and expect high-quality accommodation, the university must move ahead of its immediate requirements and provide for the future. New academic buildings are planned, often with a mixture of research and teaching functions, but now the search for external funding, including matching funding, has become commonplace, although highly extravagant in terms of staff time and effort. A development programme, with professional external consultants' advice, will over time bring in much-needed discretionary funds. As well as being intrinsically important, all these post-crisis positive developments have had a significant effect on staff morale and confidence; intangible assets that had to be conserved even in the darkest days of the recovery period.

This chapter began with an account of Lancaster's founding years, and the context of the university sketched there continues to be relevant for the future. Lancaster's relative geographical isolation and distance from major urban centres will, for example, continue to condition what actions for future growth are feasible. Similarly, the habits of a close-knit and mutually supportive community, combined with an ingrained habit of frugality, served the university well in its period of crisis and will do so in the future. The key to solving the crisis of 1995–6 was the resolve to face the reality of the problem, the centralist and top-down application of remedies combined with openness and frankness across the university and the rapidity and energy with which the recovery plan was formulated and its implementation begun even before formal approval was complete.

Thus the university, under its fifth vice-chancellor, who took up his post in October 2002, must continue to balance its international, national and regional roles. It must turn from a preoccupation with cost-cutting to a greater emphasis on acquiring additional sources of net income for its own future investment. It must harness its own intellectual property towards developments that carry with them patents, royalties and licence patents, and it will doubtless venture into new areas of academic activity. Above all, it must grow from its own established strengths and embedded characteristics to play its leading and distinctive role in UK higher education.

Notes

1   The review is popularly known as the CRILL report and is referred to as such in this chapter.
2   Pro-Chancellor's opening report to the Council of the University of Lancaster, 4 October 1996 (minute CO.96/78; document: AR/96/1567).
3   Minutes of the meeting of the Court of the University of Lancaster, 9 February 2002, p. 5 (document: AR/2002/245).

4

HOW ONE MAN WOVE A KIND OF MAGIC IN EALING

Lucy Hodges

Background

The editors of this volume were very keen to include a chapter on the crisis at Thames Valley University (TVU). Unfortunately, over the period when the book was being written it was still unclear what the final outcome would be for that university. In a letter to one of the editors in November 2000, Professor Ken Barker, the new vice-chancellor of Thames Valley University, wrote, 'There are still deep-seated problems to be solved at TVU: the expected turbulence in the higher education sector is likely to make funding solutions more difficult and 2002 is the year that the QAA [Quality Assurance Agency] is intending to carry out its next Institutional Review.' In early July 2001, Professor Barker still had his doubts, stating in another letter, 'it would also still be unwise to say anything that is predicated on success having been achieved or being sustainable at this Institution. Some day it will make an interesting case study but there are too many issues that remain on the desk – either pending or unresolved – at this time.'

Initially crestfallen, the editors were delighted when only a few days after Professor Barker had (understandably) declined to contribute, they read an article in the *Independent* about Thames Valley University by the renowned education journalist Lucy Hodges. It appeared that Ms Hodges had been able to penetrate Professor Barker's defences and the result was an informative and interesting double-page spread under the title at the head of this chapter. Consequently, with the kind permission of Ms Hodges and the Syndication Senior Executive at the *Independent*, the following article is reprinted from the *Independent* of 19 July 2001. It would seem that

although the future for TVU may still be uncertain, Professor Barker is
giving it his best shot.

Thames Valley University was failing badly. Then Professor Ken Barker was sent in to revive its fortunes

Key dates in Thames Valley's history
1960s: Freddie Mercury, Pete Townshend and Ronnie Wood attend
Ealing School of Art, part of Ealing College.
1990s: Ealing College, Thames Valley College in Slough, and
Queen Charlotte's College of Healthcare merge.
1991: London College of Music joins the three institutions. Later,
all four became the Polytechnic of West London.
1992: The Polytechnic of West London becomes Thames Valley
University.
1997: Newspaper stories appear about Thames Valley dumbing-
down degrees. An inquiry is mounted.
1998: A report finds Thames Valley wanting. Mike Fitzgerald, the
Vice-Chancellor, is forced to resign.
1999: Professor Kenneth Barker takes over as Vice-Chancellor.
2002: Student target numbers are met and Professor Barker's
strategy bears fruit.

Two-and-a-half years ago, Thames Valley University was on its knees.
The university, which in a former incarnation had educated pop
singers Freddie Mercury of Queen and Pete Townshend of The Who,
was broke, haemorrhaging students and declared to be failing. In fact,
its very future was at stake.

The news sent shock waves through the university system. Were
other places in a similar shambles, people wondered. Thames Valley
University's flamboyant, earringed Vice-Chancellor, Mike Fitzgerald,
had a gun pointed at his head and was forced out. And a 'hit squad'
was parachuted in to safeguard standards.

What has happened since? The answer is that the university is
slowly and painfully being turned round by Professor Ken Barker, 67,
who was retiring as the successful founding Vice-Chancellor of De
Montfort University in 1999 and was persuaded to take over the ailing
Thames Valley instead. With a mixture of hard work and hard-
headedness, he is reviving the institution.

Systems have been put in place to guarantee quality. Departments
that weren't attracting enough students were axed, staff laid off and
applied areas built up. Like one or two other former polytechnics,
Thames Valley, which extends from Ealing in West London to Slough

in Berkshire, is now the ultimate vocational university. It has no humanities, science or engineering departments. Instead, it comprises three huge faculties: professional studies, including business, management and law, tourism, hospitality and leisure; music, media and creative technologies; and health and human sciences.

'There were some big battles,' recalls Professor Barker matter-of-factly. 'Quite a lot of purging of staff went on. There was a first wave when about 70 academic staff were made redundant. Then a second wave had to be laid off. And the redundancy terms were not as good for them as they were for the first lot.'

The crisis began in 1997 when the university was accused of 'dumbing down' standards to pass more students. Those accusations were not substantiated but investigators from the Quality Assurance Agency were sufficiently worried to launch a full-scale inquiry. The report of that inquiry was devastating. It catalogued a litany of failings: disbelieving external examiners, a disaffected workforce, poor management, weak communications and serious questions about standards.

Sir William Taylor, the university troubleshooter who sorted out Huddersfield University when its boss ran into trouble, was brought in to restore order. Together with Quentin Thompson, the higher education consultant who used to work for PricewaterhouseCoopers (PwC), he produced an action plan, based on an analysis of which subjects were viable and which weren't.

One of the first disciplines to be chopped was linguistics, the university's pride and joy. It had secured a top grade 5 in the 1996 research assessment exercise and brought immense kudos to Thames Valley. (Very few new universities have a grade 5 in any subject.) But the hit squad decided that, although the high rating gave the university several hundred thousand pounds from the Higher Education Funding Council (HEFCE), that money was not enough to justify an uneconomic course.

The subject did not attract enough students. Therefore, it was closed and some of the academics transferred to King's College London; the remainder were made redundant.

The complicated management structure, which left students confused, was streamlined. The system that gave each student a director of studies who didn't necessarily have any knowledge of the student's subjects was abolished. And the New Learning Environment, one of Mike Fitzgerald's most ambitious reforms, which emphasized student learning rather than lecturers' teaching, was reformed.

The action plan contained targets for student numbers that underpinned the budget calculations. The problem was that those targets were over optimistic. 'In 1999, when I walked in, I found that the targets had not been hit and we were looking at a £5m deficit for that year,' says Professor Barker. 'My task was to produce another plan.'

The new Vice-Chancellor reworked all the sums, revising them downwards. The university began to retrench more seriously. All humanities and social science subjects were cut. Professor Barker reduced the student numbers target by 10 per cent. 'We projected through the next four to five years on a more modest basis,' he says. 'We still had a big hole in the balance sheet and we had no reserves.'

Something had to give. Professor Barker decided there was only one thing for it; he would have to sell part of the land the university owned in Slough. The sale of this land is now in process and the proceeds will go towards plugging the £5 million-plus funding gap and upgrading the building that it is retaining in Slough.

The strategy seems to have worked. In the last academic year, 2000–1, the university met its recruitment targets. Today, student numbers stand at 25,700, including full- and part-timers, open learners, undergraduates and postgraduates. That is 2 per cent more than it wanted. And in the past year the university made a surplus on its operating costs.

The immediate crisis has been overcome and the Vice-Chancellor now has to make Thames Valley thrive. This is no easy task. The funding mechanisms work against new universities because they reward research much more than teaching. Moreover, the introduction of the market place into higher education means that less popular universities, the former polytechnics, have difficulty attracting students. London institutions are in particular difficulty because there are so many of them. Then there is the student drop-out rate which stands at 30 per cent.

Professor Barker is taking a leaf out of his De Montfort experience. That university has successfully raised its profile in research. The Vice-Chancellor is determined Thames Valley should do the same.

Without ground-breaking research universities can't build up a lucrative funding stream from HEFCE. Nor can they establish effective links with companies. 'Having been at De Montfort I know it takes 10 years to embed a research culture,' says Professor Barker.

A shrewd and quiet operator, the new Vice-Chancellor is clever with people. Mike Fitzgerald's regime was beset with rows with the lecturers' union, NATFHE (National Association of Teachers in Further and Higher Education). When the crisis erupted, NATFHE was refusing to give the students their marks. Professor Barker says the changes have been accomplished with no industrial disruption . . . 'NATFHE are representing the interests of their members in the right kind of way,' he adds.

Slowly, the word is spreading that Thames Valley has emerged from its crisis. That is helping with another of the Vice-Chancellor's aims, which is to attract some big names from outside. Professor David Green, who runs the business school at Leeds Metropolitan University, has been hired as Pro Vice-Chancellor and Dean of the Faculty of Professional Studies.

Last week it was announced that Sir William Stubbs, retiring as rector of the London Institute (the umbrella institution for the London art colleges), is to be the university's new Chancellor. The ultimate education mandarin, Sir William has held a succession of top education jobs, including chief executive of the Inner London Education Authority and the Polytechnics and Colleges Funding Council. He is currently chairman of the Qualifications and Curriculum Authority.

'I have seen how education institutions are dynamic and can change,' he says. 'Nothing is inevitable. You're either going down or going up. What makes the difference is human intervention. Thames Valley ran into exceedingly choppy waters and some people thought the ship would founder. It is to the enormous credit of Ken Barker that he was prepared to go in and face up to the challenge. I have watched him grapple with that. It was not easy for him in the early days but it is clear that the university is now on a new course.' Student morale has revived, according to Claire Pardoe, student union president. Students are flocking to the new cool courses of digital arts, animation and video production. But experts are cautious, asking what can be the long-term future of a university which has experienced such problems in a market as volatile as higher education. The University of North London is merging with London Guildhall; and the University of East London may join them shortly. 'Will Thames Valley be with us in five years' time?' asked one.

Tom Wilson, head of NATFHE's universities department, says: 'I think the jury's still out. The university has certainly turned itself around and made great strides but it is by no means out of the wood.'

5

SOUTHAMPTON INSTITUTE
Roger Brown

Introduction

This account of the crisis at Southampton Institute between 1989 and 1999 covers four main areas:

- a description of the institute and the historical context;
- an analytical account of how the crisis arose and how it was resolved;
- a description of how the institute recovered;
- some reflections on the structural questions raised.

The Institute

Southampton Institute is a major higher education college, one of the largest of its kind outside the universities. In 2001–2 there were 10,000 full-time equivalent students, 8,800 full-time students and 1,150 part-time students. The Institute offered 96 degree courses, 53 Higher National Diplomas/Higher National Certificates and 29 postgraduate programmes. By August 2001, 71 (56 PhD and 15 MPhil) students had obtained research degrees and there were 108 current research degree registrations. The institute offered a wide span of programmes, ranging from computing and systems engineering through maritime studies, law, business and management, finance, marketing, sport, tourism and leisure, human sciences to media studies and communications and visual art and design.

The institute's annual turnover in 2001–2 was expected to be £56 million. The institute is heavily dependent upon Funding Council grants, though the Warsash Maritime Centre, a world famous centre of maritime education and training, provides a useful source of diversified income. The institute offers the awards of the Nottingham Trent University under an accreditation agreement first entered into in 1992. Since August 2000, the institute has been organized into three faculties: the faculty of technology, the Southampton Business School and the faculty of media, arts and society. The great majority of programmes are vocational and the institute has one of the best records for graduate employment in the sector. It also takes widening participation seriously, with about a quarter of students entering without any formal entry qualifications. The institute is located in the centre of the city of Southampton and plays an important part in the affairs of Southampton and the surrounding city region. The institute is in many respects a model of a 'modern' higher education institution (Southampton Institute 2001).

The historical context

Developments at Southampton Institute between 1989 and 1999 cannot be understood without reference to the policy environment. This was in three phases.

Prior to 1989 the institute belonged to its local authority, Hampshire County Council. The institution had no legal identity and could not enter into contracts or employ staff. This was not purely a question of form. As a matter of policy, while the institute was allowed, from the mid-1980s onwards, to run part-time degree programmes, the county council's policy was to restrict the development of full-time degree programmes to the then Portsmouth Polytechnic. That institution was similarly constrained in status even though it reputedly came close to obtaining a university title in 1962. As a result, the bulk of the institute's higher-level work consisted of courses preparing part-time students for professional qualifications like the Chartered Insurance Institute and the Institute of Bankers; just over a decade later, these qualifications, and the related professions, have virtually ceased to exist.

The government's decision, announced in the White Paper *Higher Education Meeting the Challenge* (DES 1987), to free the polytechnics and major higher education colleges from local authority control through their becoming corporations in their own right (technically the Inner London polytechnics were already separate companies) marked the start of the second phase. The aim now, confirmed in the White Paper *Higher Education: A New Framework* (DES 1991) announcing the government's intention – realized the following year

– to enable the polytechnics and certain other institutions to obtain a university title, was to expand the system by whatever means came to hand. Universities and colleges were to become more enterprising and less risk averse, and as part of this the majority of the governors of the new corporations were to be 'persons appearing to the appointing authority, to have experience of, and have shown a capacity in, industrial, commercial or employment matters on the practice of any profession.' This was part of a broader neo-liberal trend towards making universities and colleges (and other educational institutions) as much like commercial businesses as possible.

The era of headlong expansion, of which the institute was perhaps the most spectacular example, came to an abrupt end with the slamming on of the brakes and the capping of student numbers from 1993. This coincided with a slowing of demand as the improvement in post-16 staying on rates (a function largely of the introduction of the General Certificate of Secondary Education) began to tail off. As a valuable HEFCE (2001) publication shows, since the mid-1990s overall demand for higher education has been flat (though the publication fails to acknowledge the impact of the introduction of a student contribution to tuition costs and the abolition of maintenance grants from 1998 – the government must be the only government in history to deny that raising the price of a good or service can have any impact on the demand for that good or service!).

This economic retrenchment was accompanied by an academic reaction as concerns began to be raised about British universities' academic standards. This began with the then Secretary of State's visit to Malaysia and Singapore in early 1994 (where he was assailed by complaints from his hosts about the tactics and claims British universities and colleges were resorting to in order to recruit students and partner institutions) and culminated in the much more elaborate regulatory framework within which UK universities and colleges now find themselves (Brown 2002). As part of this process, the rules for obtaining degree awarding powers and a university title were tightened first under the Higher Education Quality Council (of which the author was chief executive from 1993 to 1997) and then, more drastically, under HEQC's successor body, the Quality Assurance Agency for Higher Education (QAA). This third phase continues to this day.

Background to the crisis

The crisis at Southampton Institute was essentially a crisis of governance. There were (again) three main phases:

- Between 1988 (when the legislation removing the polytechnics and colleges from local authority control was enacted) and the end of 1993. This period saw rapid expansion but also a consolidation of power within the institute. It also saw the failure of the institute's early ambitions to achieve accreditation from the Council for National Academic Awards (CNAA) and polytechnic status.
- Between early 1994 and early 1996. This saw the institute's attempt to respond to the external changes which called its previous strategy of expansion into question, the failure of those attempts and the first signs of opposition to the institute director.
- From early 1996 to the middle of 1997. This was the crisis that led to the institute director's retirement in August 1997.

From 1988 to 1993

The crucial events during this period were:

- The establishment of governance arrangements that, as with other institutions with similar constitutions, gave considerable power to the institute director.
- The appointment of an institute director who made no secret of his intention to develop the institute on commercial lines as an entrepreneurial institution and who reorganized the institute into a small number of 'divisions' to bring this about.
- The establishment, at about the same time, of an effective triumvirate (institute director, chairman, vice-chairman of governors) that took most of the key decisions.
- The grouping of divisions into three 'schools' under permanent directors reporting directly to the institute director.
- The agreement by the board of governors to a strategy to achieve CNAA accreditation and polytechnic size in the shortest possible time.
- The consequent expansion to 10,270 students by the end of 1993, compared with 4521 full-time equivalent at the time of incorporation. At the same time the institute began to develop the characteristics of a university, including the first professorial titles.
- The development of halls of residence, which would eventually provide bed spaces for over 3000 students, albeit at a considerable cost in terms of financing.
- The ending of the polytechnic title by the Department of Education and Science and the rejection by the CNAA of the institute's bid for accreditation as an institution able to award the Council's degrees with a minimum of Council oversight.

- The reduction in the number of separate governors' committees from five to two (audit and resources), together with a switch to sending board members resumes of committee meetings, rather than full minutes (these changes were later reversed).

From early 1994 to early 1996

During this period, a number of initiatives began that were to become issues in the crisis in 1996–7. The main developments were:

- The rejection by the Privy Council Office, on HEQC advice, of the institute's application for its own degree awarding powers.
- The initiation of a series of ventures designed to generate additional revenue, following the government's decision to impose controls on the further expansion of home and EU student numbers and the British Council's promotion of overseas expansion by UK universities and colleges. The most significant of these were a free-standing income-generating company to be known as STAR and a series of overseas franchises and campus developments in Ireland, Greece, Spain and India.
- The renewal of the institute director's contract.
- The beginnings of frustration as the developing academic community began to challenge the leadership and style, and as changes in the external environment made continued expansion less viable. Pressure came, particularly from the middle management level, to consolidate, decentralize the power base and create a culture of collegiality.
- A further internal restructuring under which the three directors of school were to take on cross-institute responsibilities so that there were now to be six functional directors besides the institute director, making a directorate of seven. Schools would be dissolved and the heads of the nine existing divisions would become deans. The divisions were to be retitled as 'faculties' and were to have greater autonomy.
- The first signs of governor dissent at the establishment of the campus in Athens, and the first indications of staff resentment at the institute director's management style.
- The institutional quality audit by HEQC in November 1995, though the outcomes of this were not fully clear until the following spring.

By early 1996, serious problems had begun to emerge. Staff were exhausted from the demands of expansion and needed time to reflect and consolidate within the promised collegiate culture. It was widely perceived that the change of name from 'division' to 'faculty' had been superficial and that no real devolution of authority had ever been intended. Those who would have preferred to concentrate on embedding academic quality further in order to secure taught degree awarding powers feared that their work would be put in jeopardy by the overseas ventures. At this point, the institute director suddenly announced to his senior management team that he had decided upon yet another management restructuring, hardly a year since the previous change, and without any consultation with the deans with whom he had just spent two days in 'team-building'. This proved to be the catalyst for the crisis.

From early 1996 to early 1998

The main occurrences during this period were:

- The first press coverage of the management of the institute, particularly relating to the Athens campus. This adverse media coverage continued almost unabated throughout the period and reached a crescendo in the spring of 1997.
- The receipt of the HEQC audit report containing a number of negative points aimed mainly at the overseas franchises, and the institute director's consideration of attempting to prevent its publication.
- The first votes of no confidence in the institute director on the part of staff and students.
- The agreement by the board of governors to commission a communications audit subsequently undertaken by Professor Geoffrey Hall, former Director of Brighton Polytechnic. The report, in November 1996, was highly critical of the institute director's management style and the frequent academic and administrative reorganizations. Parallel concerns were expressed by two governors, one of them an academic board nominee. There was also criticism of crucial decisions, in particular the creation of a new building in East Park Terrace, being made by a small group of governors in resources committee.
- The voluntary redundancy of the director of corporate development, it being widely believed in the institute that this was the outcome of his having led a deputation of directors to tell the chairman that they had lost confidence in the institute director.
- The decision to withdraw from the Athens campus.

- Two special HEFCE audits of internal controls at the institute prompted by complaints made to the Funding Council. While the complaints proved groundless, the Funding Council was concerned about the press damage these allegations were doing to the reputation of the institute.
- The decision of the National Audit Office (NAO) to institute inquiries into the planning and conduct of the Institute's overseas operations.
- The hiring in March 1997 by the institute director of a former police chief superintendent in an attempt to identify the authors of a satirical magazine, based on *Private Eye*, circulating at the institute. The title *The Dunghill* was a deliberate parody of the institute director's magazine *The Molehill*.
- The institute director's failed attempt to further restructure the institute from nine faculties to six.
- The decision of the board of governors in May 1997, following a confidential exchange with the HEFCE chief executive, to offer the institute director the opportunity to retire early and the acceptance by the institute director of that offer with effect from 31 August 1997.
- The appointment of Professor Tim Wheeler, director for academic quality, as acting institute director pending the appointment of a permanent successor (this was agreed at the board meeting on 9 July 1997 and confirmed by the board on 1 October).
- The resignation of the chair of governors.
- The appointment in January 1998, as institute director, of Dr Roger Brown, previously chief executive of the Higher Education Quality Council, the appointment being taken up on 1 April 1998.

The NAO report

In December 1998 the NAO published its report on overseas operations, governance and management at Southampton Institute between 1994 and 1997. The overall messages were that:

- Greater care and thought should have gone into the planning and management of the overseas operations in the context of an appropriate overall institutional strategy.
- Greater information and explanation should have been provided to governors and other stakeholders in the context of a more open and trusting relationship between the institute director, the chairman and vice-chairman of governors, other governors and the institution as a whole.

As regards governance and management, the main findings were:

- There was a lack of cohesiveness in the board of governors, and within the former senior management team.
- The composition of board subcommittees meant that effective power within the institute was concentrated in a small group of individuals.
- The Funding Council's first audit report was not submitted for consideration to the institute's audit committee.
- Some governors expressed concern that they were not always sufficiently involved in strategic decision-making or informed about significant developments at the institute.
- There were problems in the relationship between the board of governors and the former institute director.
- There was an absence of comprehensive independent review in cases of concern raised by staff at the institute which related to, or involved, the former institute director.
- Clerking arrangements for the audit committee were inappropriate, being in the hands of the director, resources;
- Some of the legal advice sought, and legal action taken, was not an appropriate use of institute funds.
- The institute did not take legal advice on the potential liability prior to issuing writs against certain newspapers.

I deal below with the steps taken by the institute to respond to these findings.

The Public Accounts Committee

The NAO report was the subject of a hearing by the House of Commons Public Accounts Committee in early 1999. In its subsequent report the committee echoed and endorsed the NAO conclusions. In particular it reported:

Evidence from events at Southampton Institute and other cases in both the higher and further education sectors raises deep-seated concerns about the standard of governance in institutions. The Department and the Funding Council have taken a number of steps in the light of the Nolan and Dearing reports, and specific failures at institutions, to improve their guidance to institutions and to monitor its implementation. It is now essential that effective action is taken to improve governance immediately. In particular, we recommend a fundamental re-appraisal of training arrangements for governors and a stronger lead by the Funding Council in delivering training and ensuring that it is effective.

(Public Accounts Committee 1999: i)

The steps taken by the institute to respond to the criticisms of governance and management

Between the autumn of 1997 and early 1999 the institute took a number of steps to try to ensure that the issues that had led to the crisis of governance could not recur. Overall, these steps were designed to ensure that the governing body was able to act collectively to discharge its responsibilities under the instrument and articles, particularly in relation to overall strategy. The main changes were:

- Clearer and fuller elaboration, within the governing body's terms of reference, of its various statutory responsibilities.
- An increase in the size of the governing body by two members: one an additional external co-option, the other a co-option from among the ex-officio members of the academic board.
- A strengthening of the membership of the audit committee and the restatement of the principle that governors serving on that committee should not serve on any other.
- A separation of the roles of clerk to the governors and director of resources, with the former being taken over by the institute's registrar.
- A more systematic approach to recruitment, selection and training of governors and allocation to committees.

The institute also took a number of steps to improve communications between the board, its committees, the academic board and its committees, and the institute community as a whole, including through the institution of a governors' annual report. The effectiveness of these steps was acknowledged and confirmed in two HEFCE audits in March 1998 and June 1999.

The turnaround

I first learned of the problems at the institute as chief executive of HEQC at the time of the council's audit in November 1995. I also became aware of the Funding Council's interests and concerns but it was not until I became principal (one of my first acts was to ask the chair of governors to agree to this title in place of 'institute director') that I became aware of the depth of the fissures that had emerged, and even today those fissures have not entirely disappeared. If there is one message I take from the crisis at the institute it is that serious wounds of the kind that the institute inflicted upon itself take a long while to heal.

Before describing the steps the institute took following my appointment to get itself back on track, I would like to acknowledge the work done in the interim by the acting institute director Tim Wheeler (now principal of Chester College) and the late Michael Andrews, who became chair in October 1997. Together with Bill Cutting, vice chair from October 1997 and chairman from August 1998, they introduced a calmer atmosphere and a more normal way of doing things. It was during this time that the institute made, with Funding Council support, the changes in its governance arrangements that have been described.

Management style

In his communications audit, Professor Hall referred to the need for a change of management style, one very different from that which had been so effective at the time of rapid expansion:

> It is suggested that in a process of consolidation a new style of leadership is required . . . [one] which requires effective corporate management where a Principal, his supporting Directors and Deans are able to work as a team to drive the Institute to its next stage of development.
>
> (Hall 1996: 24)

Professor Hall added:

> It is sad to say that in response to the question 'why do you not speak up and express your views forcefully on academic matters or on institutional matters?', the response given by a large number of staff from the most senior to the most junior was fear.
>
> Fear of the consequences of speaking out. Thus communication of views that might be helpful to the work of the Institute may not be occurring. It is essential that academic staff at all levels feel that there is an atmosphere pervading in the Institute which welcomes their contribution to debate.
>
> (Hall 1996: 24)

Similarly, the second special HEFCE audit report commented on the need to move towards a more open, consultative and participative management style.

From the start, I made it clear that I favoured such a style. In accordance with all my previous experience, the principles on which I operated were, and are:

- Policy-making and determination should be reserved to the institute's collective organs of governance: the governing body, the academic board and its committees, and the senior management team and its committees.
- As far as possible, decisions should be made on the basis of consensus, and only after full and open consultation, deliberation and debate.
- For those decisions to be effective, those making them need the fullest information, including information about alternative options and policies and the risks associated with them. It is cardinal that everyone knows what is going on and that no one feels at a disadvantage because someone else has, or appears to have, information which they themselves do not have.
- The implementation of policies should be devolved to the lowest possible level so that decisions can be taken by those who know most about the issues concerned and a full sense of ownership and responsibility is achieved.
- There should at all times be the best possible communication about decisions being taken and the reasons.

Beyond this general approach I took the following specific steps to help to refocus the institute. At a management conference in April 1998 I set out my view of the challenges facing the institute and the options before it. I made little secret of the fact that I thought that the institute had made some poor strategic choices in the mid-1990s. I proposed a strategic review and plan that would identify the objectives to be achieved by the institute in the next few years.

At the same time, in order to determine the institute's readiness for degree awarding powers, I conducted a quality audit of the institution with the help of two highly experienced HEQC auditors. This confirmed my impression that there were no serious quality weaknesses at the institute but a number of improvements were identified, in particular the need to look critically at the remaining franchises and the need to refocus our academic development activities by creating a new academic development service.

In July 1998 I launched a consultative document on future strategic objectives. The document described the context and the options facing the institute. It was the subject of wide consultation across the institute.

Final decisions on the new plan were taken by a new strategic plan committee, which was established specifically to advise the governors and the academic board on overall strategy. This reflected my wish to create a better and closer relationship between the governors and senior academic staff as well as the need to have as wide and thorough a debate as possible of the strategic choices facing the institute post-Dearing. The strategic plan committee has continued to meet regularly to review progress in achieving the strategic objectives.

Following agreement on the objectives, the faculties were asked, in early 1999, to produce plans showing how the objectives would be achieved. The plans were quite unrealistic. The transition team, the group advising on the development of the plan, took the view, with which I reluctantly agreed, that the existing faculty structure was not fit to deliver our ambitious objectives. After further consultation, therefore, the strategic plan committee and governors agreed in the summer of 1999 to the introduction, from the beginning of the 2000–1 academic year, of a new three faculty structure. There was also to be a substantial reduction in the number of management posts within the new faculties as compared with the old ones.

One of the major reasons for the restructuring was the need to devolve more. On taking up my appointment I was appalled at the extent to which decision-making was still centralized. For similar reasons I took the opportunity to reduce the size of the directorate (principal plus deputies) from four to three (after Tim Wheeler was appointed at Chester) and from three to two (when the then director, resources retired in the summer of 2000). It was seven at its largest. In the same spirit, the number of separate services has been reduced from thirteen to ten.

These efforts at confidence building were not confined to the institute. I also embarked on a major exercise to restore confidence in the institute externally, drawing upon the contacts and networks I had established as chief executive of HEQC, chief executive of the Committee of Directors of Polytechnics and secretary of the Polytechnics and Colleges Funding Council (since 1990). One product of this was my election as vice-chair of SCOP (the Standing Conference of Principals, the representative body for the higher education colleges) in November 1999.

An early, though not entirely welcome, opportunity to do so was provided by the National Audit Office. Most of the information upon which the report was based was supplied by Professor Wheeler but as the institute accounting officer I was responsible for signing the report off and, of course, for explaining publicly what the institute had done to deal with the problems that had arisen.

This culminated in my appearance, on 22 March 1999, before the House of Commons Public Accounts Committee, along with the chief executive of the Funding Council and the permanent secretary to the department. This is not an experience I would recommend. I have often pondered on the irony of the fact that of the several institutions that were subject to NAO scrutiny over this period I was the only head who was actually called to give evidence, yet I was the only one who had not been the subject of any of the reports. While this was a considerable claim on my time, as well as the source of yet more unhelpful publicity for the institute, it was also an opportunity to understand and get on top of the issues that had caused the crisis, so giving me a better understanding of what needed to be done to restore confidence.

It is still too soon to say whether the institute has entirely recovered from its crisis. However, an external view of some weight was broadly positive. The August 2000 QAA *Quality Audit Report* concluded:

> The critical reports of the National Audit Office . . . damaged the Institute's public image and its self-esteem. However, these reports led to significant change in institutional governance and management under a new Principal, appointed in May 1998. A newly created committee, with representatives from both the Academic Board and the Board of Governors, is illustrative of attempts to harmonise governance and management. The major purpose of recent organisational changes has been to give the Institute a new vision, moving away from an institution based on central control and direction to one with devolved responsibility for academic standards and other matters, based on concepts of shared leadership, openness and collegiality. The Institute has withdrawn from most of its overseas franchise provision, concentrating instead on local collaborative relationships that appear to be well managed . . .
>
> The progressive devolution of operational responsibility, and the move from eight to three faculties represents a clear change in strategic direction in the management of the Institute. In principle, such an approach should foster improved ownership of quality and standards matters amongst staff and should also enable central institutional bodies to give greater attention to strategic appraisal and development.
>
> (QAA 2000: 12, 13)

Under the points for commendation, the report mentioned: 'the Institute's strategic planning processes have sought to encourage a new organisational culture and an equalisation of resource allocation intended to have benefits of quality assurance and enhancement' (QAA 2000: 14).

Conclusions

In this final section I want to comment on some of the issues that arose from the institute and other broadly similar cases.

When I appeared before the House of Commons Public Accounts Committee, one of the questions I anticipated was: 'what can you say to reassure us that this sort of thing will never again happen at Southampton Institute?' While I would have been able to provide such reassurances in respect of the institute, I am less sanguine about other institutions with similar governance arrangements, for reasons set out at greater length in an article published in *Perspectives* in 2001. In the article I commented:

> If there is one common feature running through these [cases] it is the difficulty which these institutions had in controlling the behaviour of a strong chief executive who was often closely associated with a small group of key Governors who may have by-passed a largely supine Governing Body, many of whom were not sufficiently knowledgeable either about higher education matters or about their own rights and responsibilities as members of the supreme decision making body of a higher education institution.
>
> (Brown 2001a: 44)

However, this is only one of the problems with the current arrangements in the new universities and colleges. The others are:

- The representativeness or otherwise of the governing body.
- The wisdom or otherwise of the separation between matters reserved to governors, on the one hand, and those reserved to academic board, on the other.
- Whether there should be some independent regulator to help ensure effective governance across the sector.

I therefore proposed that we move to a new system of governance in these institutions. This would have the following main features. First, governing bodies should continue at their present size but should be quite explicitly representative of the three main sets of interests in the institution: staff; students (past and present); and local and regional communities. Second, each of these groups should constitute not only an electoral college for nominating governors but also a forum that the principal should be required to consult on major issues, and that could also summon them to answer questions, or produce reports, on specific matters. Third, each 'college', as well as the main board, would have annual meetings at which the governing body/principal would make a report on how they had exercised their stewardship over the past year. These meetings should be public.

The division of labour between the governing body and the principal would remain broadly as it is now. There would be no ring-fencing of academic matters but academic freedom would be safeguarded, including through recourse to an outside authority if necessary (see below). There would be a policy and resources committee able to cover the full range of issues. To avoid any conflict of interests, the principal would not be a member of the governing body.

These arrangements would be subject to regular scrutiny by a new organization, the Higher Education Audit Commission, whose main job would be to report on the effectiveness with which institutions were achieving their objectives. The commission would combine the evaluation functions of the Higher Education Funding Councils, the QAA and other regulatory bodies. The commission would provide a means of independent consideration of complaints or appeals against decisions of the governing body, as well as independent advice to governors about their powers where needed. It could also train governors. This aspect of the arrangements is set out more fully in Brown (2001b).

Together, these proposals, if implemented, would have three main advantages over current ones. First, there would be a single evaluation regime covering all aspects of institutional activities without the artificial separations that exist at present, e.g. between 'academic' and 'resource' matters. Second, the regime would focus on the basic mechanisms of effectiveness at institutional (and sub-institutional) level, and in particular on institutional leadership and management. Third, the regime would be administered by a single body independent of government and its agencies as well as institutions.

These ideas are not as radical as they sound. For example, the institutional accreditation method operated by the regional accrediting agencies in the United States already includes governance as one of the aspects scrutinised. The QAA already looks at the governance of institutions seeking their own degree awarding powers or a university title, and institutional governance and management is also dealt with, explicitly or implicitly, in audit reports. It is also the case that the new quality assurance method that is being finalized at the time of writing will concentrate on evaluating the effectiveness of quality mechanisms at institutional level, which includes not only the functioning of the academic board/senate but also the council/governing body as it relates to academic and educational matters. Finally, the representative bodies for UK higher education – Universities UK and the SCOP – have just accepted in principle the notion of an independent advisor to adjudicate on student complaints against institutions. We are therefore already beginning to move in the direction pointed to by my proposals, though much still remains to be done.

Envoi

The crisis at Southampton Institute between 1989 and 1999 was a major setback for this excellent institution of higher education but it was also a seminal event for the sector. While the institute has certainly learnt from the experience, so that in nearly all respects it is now a model of good governance, there remain some important messages for the sector. I hope that this case study and others in this collection will assist with this reflective process.

Acknowledgements

The author wishes to acknowledge and place on record the helpful assistance he has received from Dr Jeff Richards, formerly dean of social science at the institute, in compiling this case study.

6

THE EXPERIENCE OF LONDON GUILDHALL UNIVERSITY

Roderick Floud

The Origins

Inheritance from ILEA

The origins of London Guildhall's financial crisis of 1996 lay in its inheritance from the Inner London Education Authority (ILEA), from which, as City of London Polytechnic (CLP), it had become independent in April 1989. ILEA had funded its polytechnics relatively generously but had consistently failed to solve the major problem of CLP: that it was housed in a collection of ageing buildings in the middle of one of the most expensive areas in the world. This geographical location was central to the work of the polytechnic, particularly in its historic role of training the workforce of the City of London, but successive ILEA administrations found it difficult to accept the necessary costs of fulfilling that role. One consequence was a vain search during the 1970s and 1980s, consuming much of the energy of the polytechnic and its managers, for an alternative site on which the institution could be united.

When, in 1988, ILEA found that it was to lose control of its polytechnics, it not only immediately reduced its recurrent funding to all of them but, in the case of CLP, withdrew the offer of the latest new site that had been earmarked.[1] This left the newly independent polytechnic not only without a new site but with a collection of buildings in poor condition and on short leases, negotiated on the assumption that the institution would shortly be moving from them. In 1989, several thousand students were being taught in buildings whose leases were due to terminate – without any right to renew – before the students would have finished their courses.

This first crisis in the life of the independent polytechnic led to proposals, ultimately abortive, for a merger with what was to become Anglia Polytechnic University. More positively it led, through the generosity of the City of London Corporation and the cooperation of the Polytechnics and Colleges Funding Council (PCFC), to a restructuring of the leases that secured the polytechnic's position in the City and East London. The polytechnic remained vulnerable, however, because of the size of rental payments as a proportion of its income[2] and because its buildings remained in a deplorable condition.

The early 1990s

The poor inheritance of buildings had long-lasting consequences for a number of reasons. First, far too much management time was occupied with them. Second, too much of the recurrent funding of the polytechnic had to be spent on improving their condition. Third, the problem at times seemed so intractable that it bred a sense of helplessness, a kind of 'victim mentality', within some of the staff; this inhibited efforts to diversify the income sources of the institution. Finally, it led the polytechnic management and governors to take the decision, responsible in the circumstances but deleterious in the medium term, not to expand student numbers as much as every other polytechnic, and many universities, did in the early 1990s.

Efficiency gains

Expansion of student numbers was based, in the early 1990s, on a system of bidding for additional numbers, which led inevitably to a reduction in funding per student. It also led to a growth of numbers – as institutions scrambled to increase their income by admitting more students – which ultimately so alarmed the government, because of its consequences for public expenditure on student support, that it imposed a limit on further expansion. However, government continued, through the imposition of annual 'efficiency gains', to drive down funding per student. This policy, while just supportable when the system was growing, became increasingly difficult to cope with once growth had ceased.

The situation became even worse after the decision – very welcome in other ways – to unify the higher education system and to confer the title of university on the former polytechnics. The new Higher Education Funding Council pursued the laudable aim of funding teaching provision at the same level in all institutions but, for reasons that are still obscure, this led in practice to driving down further the funding of many of the former polytechnics.[3] By 1994 or 1995, it was clear to many new university managers that the financial situation was unsustainable and that only substantial cuts in expenditure could preserve the viability of their institutions.

Redundancy and retirement costs

Universities are labour-intensive organizations, typically spending 60–65 per cent of their income on staff. The renamed London Guild-hall University was no exception, but its expenditure was squeezed further by the high and unavoidable costs of operating in or near the City of London, by significant expenditure on renovating its buildings and the difficulty – perhaps stemming from its lack of science or engineering departments – of developing alternative sources of income to that from the Funding Council. Since surveys of the physical condition of the buildings showed that expenditure on them could not be significantly reduced, it was clear that cuts in expenditure could come only from reductions in staff. This position became clear in 1993.

The university was constrained by a 'no (compulsory) redundancy' policy adopted by the governors at the time of ILEA control and, more importantly, by a natural wish not to deal badly with staff who had served the institution for many years. It therefore sought to reach agreement with the staff trade unions on a package of voluntary redundancy and early retirement measures that would, it was hoped, reduce expenditure in the medium term, although at considerable cost in the short term. An agreement was reached in 1994 and volunteers came forward in sufficient numbers. It was, however, mistakenly assumed that the cost of redundancies – in terms of future pension provisions – could be spread over a number of years. When this proved not to be the case because of accounting rules, the resultant costs and the need for substantial expenditure on main-tenance of buildings wiped out the relatively meagre cash reserves of the university and produced a deficit of £5.7 million in the income and expenditure account for the 1993–4 financial year. This was followed by a further deficit of £311,000 in the financial year 1994–5. These were significant figures in the context of an overall annual income of about £40 million at the time, particularly as a further large deficit was anticipated for 1995–6. The university had negative reserves, with the reserve position worsening rapidly.

These events coincided with a period of low morale among staff in the university, who were naturally concerned by the financial position, by abortive discussions about a merger with City University and by the uncertainty about the future of the university. There were particular concerns in the business faculty. It was suggested in 1994 that a study should be made of internal processes for communication and consultation with staff. This study was conducted by Stephen Jones, a former senior member of the management. It made a number of recommendations in 1995; among those that were implemented was that departmental councils should be established to advise heads of department.

The shape of the crisis

Forecast deficit

This situation, already difficult, was made significantly worse in the summer of 1995 by the publication of government spending plans that set out the extent of further efficiency gains that would be demanded of the higher education system in the years up to 1998. When those plans were applied to forecasting the future income of London Guildhall, and when those income projections were set against expenditure trends during a period of significant, although diminishing, wage inflation, it was clear that the university had to expect that the deficits of 1993–4 and 1994–5 would be followed by a succession of further deficits. Not only would the university be in breach of its financial agreement with the HEFCE (which prohibited more than three successive deficits) but, since its cash reserves were so low, it would rapidly become insolvent. This would have particularly serious consequences as the university, like the other former ILEA polytechnics, had been constituted as a company limited by guarantee and therefore subject to the requirements of the Companies Acts; individual governors, as directors, might potentially be liable for civil penalties including disqualification from other directorships.

Reacting to crisis

Once the forecasts of continuing deficits had been made, HEFCE was immediately notified of the seriousness of the position. At a meeting held in late summer 1995, the university agreed that it would be necessary to draw up a recovery plan that would reduce expenditure, increase income and lead towards a surplus of £2 million in 1998–9. HEFCE agreed to give some financial support to this action, but to make any further support contingent on the recommendations of the recovery plan and consequent decisions by the board of governors.

The serious nature of the financial position was communicated to the board of governors and then to the staff of the university in the autumn of 1995. There were intensive discussions with the staff trade unions, who agreed to participate in drawing up a recovery plan.

The recovery plan

Governors' working party

The board of governors established a working party, chaired by its vice-chair, John Sellars CBE, to draw up a recovery plan for submission to the board by 1 April 1996. The working party included governors, senior management staff, representatives of staff trade unions, a consultant (Quentin Thompson of Coopers and Lybrand) and an independent member from another university. The working party first commissioned Coopers and Lybrand to draw up an assessment of the financial position and forecasts, to form a basis for necessary action. Coopers and Lybrand reported their findings to the governors' working party in November 1995. They took a view – informed by the Public Expenditure Settlement of that month – that was even more pessimistic than earlier forecasts by management; it was predicted that there would be successive deficits in each year, growing to a figure of over £4 million by 1998–9. As a result, Coopers and Lybrand recommended that expenditure should be reduced by approximately £5 million over a three-year period. The working party agreed that this action should be taken and asked the officers of the university to make recommendations as to how it should be done.

The working party met regularly while the plan was being formulated. It was an extremely useful vehicle for discussion of the realities of the financial stiuation, in which the views of lay governors were reinforced by the strongly expressed concerns of the external members. The attitude of the trade union members was, throughout, responsible and reasoned; they demanded full explanations of analysis and recommendations, but accepted that action needed to be taken. They were particularly concerned that the distribution of pain should be, as far as possible, equitable. Taken all in all, the participation of trade union members was a source of great strength, possibly, indeed, the pivotal factor that led to the acceptance of the plan by the staff of the university.

Communication, publicity and anger

Much of this activity was, it should be said, undertaken in the full glare of publicity. It was understandable, though still unfortunate, that some members of the staff of the university should have sought to attribute blame for the financial position – usually to the university management – and to pursue this campaign by regularly communicating documents and views to the press. It was a matter for rueful regret, at times, that London Guildhall lies about 10 minutes' walk from the offices of the *Times Higher Education Supplement*. Press interest was heightened by the fact that, although many of the causes of the crisis were common to LGU and other universities, LGU was the first university to make them public. In addition, it was probably crucial that its low reserves meant that it had no cushion and was forced to take drastic action. The public nature of the crisis brought fears – ultimately unfounded – that student recruitment would suffer. More productively, the publicity meant that, since the nature of the crises was so public, it was possible to communicate the facts of the situation on a regular basis to members of staff. This was, in retrospect, one of the factors that led to the acceptance by the staff of the recovery plan, painful though it was to prove to be.

Communication took place through regular written briefings, a series of open meetings with staff and regular consultations with the trade unions, who also produced their own briefings. The staff meetings were at times heated, even downright unpleasant, as staff sought for an explanation of what had occurred and assurances about what was to happen. It has to be accepted that, on such occasions, anger will be directed at local management – 'the university' or 'the administration' – rather than at impersonal forces such as efficiency gains or the government or funding council. It is also probably useful for the process, even if it is somewhat at odds with the formal responsibilities of the board of governors, that they should be seen as independent, bearing little or no responsibility for the financial difficulties, yet able to take decisions for the good of the university. Anger is thus focused on senior managers, who have to be prepared to accept it and to argue patiently the reality of the crisis.

Officers' working party

While the governors commissioned and received the results of the consultants' study, which set out the size of the problem, it was for the officers to propose solutions. This was done by means of a task group, chaired initially by the then senior deputy provost and latterly by the provost, which explored the scope for savings by examining departmental budgets across the whole range of the university's work. Views were sought from all members of staff: the task group met each department and received over 330 written submissions. The group's examination of the position covered not only staffing and other expenditure in relation to income within each department, but also business processes. Particular attention was given to the role of the faculty structure, within which much of the administrative work such as registration of students was conducted. This led ultimately to the decision to recommend the abolition of the faculties and the posts of deans, the centralization of registry functions and the devolution of financial and managerial responsibility to academic departments, a package that was expected to save approximately £750,000 per annum.

There was, it has to be admitted, an element of rough justice about some of the work carried out by the officers' working party, particularly as it became more urgent, during the spring of 1996, to make recommendations that would form part of a viable recovery plan. The process inevitably revealed gaps in knowledge about income and cost structures, both current and forecast, and there was a tendency to waste time on refining information rather than taking what, inevitably, had to be 'broad-brush' decisions. Ultimately, senior managers were presented with a requirement to save certain amounts of expenditure within their areas of responsibility and told to bring back the answer within a few days; to their great credit, they all did so despite the very painful decisions they had to make. Some decisions could not be taken in this way, in particular those concerned with overall business processes and structures and with the viability of whole areas of activity.

Decisions

The recovery plan

There was, inevitably, a great deal of argument before the recovery plan was accepted by the governors' working party, including its trade union members, and recommended to the board of governors for decision on 1 April 1996. Much dissent was focused on the last element of the plan to be agreed – essentially the element that made up expenditure savings to the required level. This was the recommendation not to pay the annual increase in pay determined by national negotiation; this left pay at London Guildhall lagging slightly behind that in the rest of the new university sector, although it was always the intention – later realized – to return to parity with the rest of the sector when finances permitted.

Other than this, the main elements of the recovery plan were as follows:

- *Academic proposals:* to reduce the teaching of geography and mathematics;[4] to adjust staff–student ratios in each department to reflect income and expenditure; to allocate HEFCE research funding to those departments which had earned it.
- *Administrative proposals:* to abolish the faculty layer of administration; to integrate the library, computing, media and television services into a single academic services department; to merge the existing faculty-based registries and the Centre for Undergraduate Programmes into a single registry and to rationalize academic counselling support within the centre; to merge departments concerned with marketing, student recruitment and access work; to restructure the finance and personnel departments; to outsource a number of buildings-related functions; to raise funds for a nursery or, failing that, to close it.
- *Property proposals:* to alter some planned moves of departments and the central administration and to close and sell one outlying building; to rephase the maintenance plan; to relinquish the sports ground, hiring a replacement; to make other reductions in non-pay expenditure.

These proposals, together with the one-year pay freeze, were estimated to meet the requirement to save £5.5 million. It was thought that they would entail the redundancy of 23 academic and 61 non-teaching posts, with a further 25 posts being affected by outsourcing.

The reorganization was expected to have some significant consequences. The abolition of faculties, for example, would require a redesign of the processes of academic quality assurance, which had been based on faculties. On the non-teaching side, the number of departments fell from 17 to 11. There was, throughout the university, an emphasis on 'delayering' and on the simplification of processes and structures.

The plan was accepted by the board of governors and by HEFCE and attention turned to implementation.

Implementation

Implementation monitoring group

The governors and HEFCE were clear that careful monitoring of the implementation of the recovery plan would be required, and therefore established a group of independent and co-opted governors to meet regularly with senior university officers. This, and regular reports to officers of the funding council, also gave comfort to the council that the plan was on course and that it did not need to intervene further. Detailed implementation was the responsibility of the provost and his team, with the assistance of a consultant who drew up and monitored the project plan. HEFCE provided financial support for this post (as it had done for earlier consultancy studies), but did not otherwise allocate funds to the university for restructuring or other purposes.

Regulatory problems and redundancy

The plan envisaged a substantial number of job losses, although it was always hoped that most, if not all, could be achieved by voluntary severance. This proved to be the case, but it was necessary in a small number of departments to resort to compulsory redundancy. This process was complex and revealed a significant number of flaws in the university's procedures of dismissal, which had essentially been drawn up to deal with cases of indiscipline rather than financial exigency. In other words, they started from an assumption of a fault on the part of the person concerned, rather than the fact that a job could no longer be sustained. This was not, as it might have been in other parts of the university sector, because academic or other staff were thought to have 'tenure' except in the case of gross misconduct. It was instead because there had been a longstanding view, from the days of ILEA, that compulsory redundancy was not to be contemplated.

For the same reason, it was also necessary rapidly to devise procedures for determining the selection of people to be made redundant, although in the end the procedures were used only in a very small number of cases. The process threw into sharp relief the lack of available information held centrally or even in departments about members of academic staff, because of the agreement with the relevant trade union that the appraisal system was focused on development and its results could not be used for disciplinary or similar purposes. For this reason, academic staff in departments where it had been determined that redundancies were needed had to be asked to complete questionnaires about their job content, teaching and research and administrative tasks. Universities would be well advised to improve their record-keeping to provide objective evidence of past achievement and capability, in the unhappy event of this evidence being needed.

Outcomes

Financial results

Inevitably, the main focus of the recovery plan was on finance. In the event, the financial results achieved in the years which followed exceeded all expectations, as Table 6.1 shows. The recommendations of the plan were fundamental, but other important contributory factors were a series of changes to the workings of the finance department and an immediate concentration on cash management. The incoming finance director also insisted on a clearer approach to budgeting and to the authorization of expenditure, instituting a system of income budget-holders and expenditure budget-holders. This facilitated financial forecasting and planning, as well as being a major step towards better decision-making about new initiatives and about the cost of existing activity.

Devolution

An important principle that underlay the recovery plan was that of devolution of financial responsibility. Steps towards implementation of this principle were the abolition of the faculties and the consequent establishment of academic departments as budget centres, the creation of a single registry (in place of separate faculty registries) and the creation of an undergraduate programmes department with responsibility for the complex modular programme of undergraduate degrees. This structural change was followed by the allocation of expenditure budgets to departmental heads throughout the university.

Other structures also changed. In pursuit of the principle that 'committees don't do anything, only people make things happen', the number of university committees was significantly reduced[5] and individuals were clearly given responsibility either for achieving income targets or for expenditure targets (or both). Strategic planning was significantly altered; change began with the establishment of a

Table 6.1 Forecast and actual financial performance (£ million)

Financial year	Actual or predicted surplus (deficit) without action	Surplus (deficit) predicted in recovery plan	Actual surplus (deficit)	Closing balance on reserves predicted in recovery plan	Actual closing balance on reserves
1993–4	(5.434)			(0.897)	(0.897)
1994–5	(0.078)	(0.780)		(0.975)	(0.975)
1995–6	(1.901)	(2.314)		(3.289)	(2.084)
1996–7	(1.386)	1.959	3.308	(1.330)	1.224
1997–8	(3.682)	1.105	3.992	(0.225)	5.542
1998–9	(4.132)	0.727	1.430	(0.502)	8.737

strategic planning committee as a joint committee between the governors and the academic council, but it was quickly followed by a structure that emphasized the centrality to the process of departmental plans (later called departmental business plans) constructed within broad university policy. This was an attempt, praised by a number of external observers, to marry a top-down and a bottom-up approach to planning. It was largely successful, although recently it has been decided to locate the strategic planning role within the finance and employment committee, to emphasize the link between academic, financial and other forms of planning.

Significant change also took place within departments, as their heads began to exercise extended responsibilities. One important change, introduced as the result of the Stephen Jones report, was the establishment in the academic departments of departmental councils, chaired by an elected member of staff, who also became ex-officio a member of the academic council. These councils, and their chairs, have no executive role but they have become an important source of advice to the head of department and a good conduit for communication with staff. But probably more significant was the assumption by academic heads of management responsibilities.

Management structure and training

In the years before the recovery plan, managerial decision-making had been concentrated in what had, in polytechnic days, been known as 'the directorate'. This body underwent several changes in its membership and title, but in the mid-1990s consisted of all the senior staff, eight or nine people who were appointed by the board of governors. Although there were occasional meetings of this group with heads of departments, the principal conduit for information flows with academic departments was the three deans.

Experience during the recovery plan period suggested that a group of eight or nine was too large for effective discussion or decision-making, particularly when the deans naturally saw their role as being advocates for their faculties. It was therefore decided to institute a smaller executive group, meeting normally twice a week, consisting of the deputy provost (initially there were two such posts), vice-provost, director of finance and director of personnel. It was this smaller group that worked closely with the project manager and with the implementation monitoring group to carry out the tasks set out in the recovery plan.

It was clear, however, that the increased responsibilities to be given to heads of department under the planned devolution of budgetary responsibility required new mechanisms for consultation and discussion with them. A senior management group was therefore established, meeting monthly, and made up of all the heads of department, both academic and non-academic. Within the flatter structure made possible by the abolition of faculties, each of those heads reported directly to a member of the executive group, giving a further regular channel of communication.

Some academic heads of department expressed alarm at the extent of the management responsibilities that were being thrust upon them. This was a natural reaction, given that many of them had been appointed primarily as academic leaders, with no expectation that they would have to manage budgets running into millions of pounds. Some reacted badly even to the concept of management and objected to being referred to as managers.

In order to weld together the new senior management group and to equip all of its members with the skills that they would need, it was decided to undertake formal management training. With the aid of outside training consultants, a programme was devised which included both techniques such as project management and budget management and 'softer' skills of team building and human resource management. Every member of the senior management group and the executive group was expected to attend and did so. There were grumbles, about the individual trainers or about the exact topics, but a general agreement that the programme was enjoyable and did provide skills that were immediately useful, as well as helping to build a community of interest among the senior managers of the university.

The formal management development programme was extended, in its third year, to what came to be called – not without difficulty – middle managers. While academic heads of department soon came to accept their managerial role, some middle-ranking academic staff found such a description difficult to accept, if not actually insulting. However, the programme itself was well received. It has been transmuted over the years – partly because so many of the existing managers had received all the formal training that they thought was required – into regular management seminars, usually with outside speakers. Meanwhile, mentoring is provided as required to newly appointed heads who missed some or all of the initial programme.

One major topic of interest and discussion, during and since the period of the management programme, has been that of the exact nature of the managerial relationship between devolved budget holders and the executive group members to whom each of them reported. This was partly a philosophical debate about the nature of devolved budgets and of the locus of responsibility for achieving budgetary targets, partly a reflection on the nature of management. Initially, it was agreed that the member of the executive group should be regarded as the 'critical friend' of the head of department, reflecting earlier discussions on the nature of such a relationship between the provost and chair of governors. After some years, however, it was conceded that the appropriate term was 'line manager', reflecting the budget-holder's responsibility for achieving budgetary targets but their accountability to the line manager for that task. 'Critical friend' sounded more attractive but was actually a fudge.

These developments at university level were paralleled by similar debates and changing structures at departmental level. The establishment of departmental councils, initially feared by some heads as detracting from their authority, has proved a success, due to the good sense of the heads in working with the councils and the common sense displayed by those elected to chair the councils. Many departments, particularly the larger ones, have reacted to their increased responsibilities for budget and quality management by establishing additional posts of responsibility, sometimes known as principal lecturer plus posts, with additional pay. Job evaluation, initially introduced into the non-teaching departments, has recently been extended to the academic staff and has proved a good method of working out the requirements for numbers of staff at different levels and for assigning responsibilities to them.

These changes were all, in a sense, manifestations of a more structured and professional approach to human relations. The need for this had been realized during a time of crisis and it was for this reason that a director of personnel was recruited as a member of the executive group, having previously worked outside higher education. The perspective brought by that person to executive group discussions was invaluable, as was the calm and constructive approach to trade union negotiation that built quickly upon the relationships established during the drawing up and initial implementation of the recovery plan. Although industrial peace did not immediately break out, warfare was greatly diminished and many mutual agreements were reached.

Constructive dialogue was also the hallmark of the development of a new system of quality assurance. It was always seen as risky to abolish the faculties, which had had responsibility for quality assurance, and to give that task to individual academic departments, overseen by a quality management committee of the academic council. The risk lay in the need to meld different arrangements to suit academic disciplines as different as accountancy and musical instrument-making with the necessary rigour of a university-wide system, particularly since the entire undergraduate course programme was arranged within a modular structure. Different systems have been developed over time, but departments have worked well together and with a central quality unit and the result was judged entirely satisfactory in a continuation audit conducted in 2001. One aspect of the system was, and is, an emphasis on what has been called 'customer care', a term that has raised hackles among those who see students as partners rather than customers but that, under whatever name, is vital in a modern university.

'Warts and all'

If a discussion such as this is to be useful, it cannot be entirely about success. Of course some things went wrong or could have been done much better.

There are some obvious lessons. The first is to ensure that the regulatory framework, particularly in the area of human relations, is fit for any eventuality. It may be uncomfortable to have to work out procedures for compulsory redundancy, but it is much better to put them in place at a time when there is actually no threat of such redundancy than to have to cobble them together in an emergency. A related lesson is that managers have to be required to keep records of their dealings with staff, their assignment of work and any problems of discipline or lack of competence.

A second major lesson is that it is essential to avoid, or if necessary to ride roughshod over, the common academic tendency to procrastination. Decisions are almost always made on the basis of inadequate information and a financial forecast made on the back of an envelope is often as useful as one compiled with immense labour over several months. Another way of putting this is to say that management is about millions, or at least hundreds of thousands, of pounds and that too much detailed information about the pennies merely confuses matters.

A third lesson is that one should always be extremely sceptical about new ideas for making money. It is a common tendency in times of financial crisis in academic life to bemoan the fact that most funding comes from government and to seek out alternative sources of income. These are not actually very difficult to find; what is difficult is to make any significant money out of them. Increasing activity is much easier than improving the 'bottom line', as the transparency survey of research income and expenditure has graphically demonstrated. Part of the income forecasts in the recovery plan rested on excessively optimistic estimates of net income from a multimedia training venture, which, although contributing to the capital base of the university, has taken much longer than expected to break even in recurrent terms.

One mistake that London Guildhall University avoided, at least in large measure, was to sacrifice improvements in buildings and long-term maintenance to short-term pressures towards expenditure on staff. Spending on buildings was delayed, but it was always clear that the condition of office and teaching accommodation had to be maintained or enhanced if the university was to be able to attract and retain both staff and students. Thus significant expenditure was incurred, even during the period of the recovery plan, on the creation of the Sir John Cass Centre for Silversmithing and Jewellery, containing state-of-the-art workshops and partly funded by the Goldsmiths' Company. Since then, there have been a number of new building projects, most notably for the lottery-funded Women's Library.

Some things could definitely have been done better. It is a truism that one can never have too much communication. But carrying out the intention to communicate is always easier said than done. There will always be moments, during any crisis, when something – often to do with individuals – is simply too confidential to be discussed or made public. There is also always a tendency to be reactive, to respond to the rumours or 'Chinese whispers' that sweep around any institution and thus lose the initiative. It is better, even if it is a counsel of perfection, for communication to be concentrated in the hands of the head of the institution and a small team working with him or her, who can try to anticipate problems and take action to resolve those that occur.

Conclusion and the way forward

It is generally agreed that London Guildhall emerged stronger from the crisis of 1995–6 and from the implementation of the recovery plan. Indeed, quite a common reaction to the proposals, announced in 2001 and carried out in 2002, for a merger between London Guildhall and the University of North London was: 'Why should we throw away what we achieved with the recovery plan?' Staff who asked this question were probably thinking not as much of the financial results, good though those were, as of the devolved departmental structure and the sense of greater control over their own area of work. It is interesting that this feeling was so strong, despite the continued pressures of funding and student recruitment during the years since 1996.

Because of the success of the years since the recovery plan, the merger proposals of 2001–2 were not the product of financial crisis, as has been the case with a number of mergers in higher education. They reflected, instead, the sense that much had been achieved since 1996 but that the capacity and potential of the university were still constrained, still unrealized. In part, this was because, despite the achievements of the recovery plan, the university remained too small and too lacking in capital resources to be able to generate surpluses that would allow it to invest and branch out in new directions.

It remains to be seen how London Metropolitan University fares in the ever-changing world of British higher education. For those who lived through the recovery plan, however, the merger is a further step in serving a student body that still experiences great disadvantage yet has such great potential. It is this aim that justified the steps taken in 1996 – painful though they were – and that now justifies the creation of one of the largest, and it is hoped one of the strongest, British universities.

Notes

1   The Shoreditch site now occupied by Hackney Community College.
2   These payments, known as 'inherited liabilities' were greater for City of London Polytechic than for any other polytechnic.
3   It is likely that this was an unintended consequence of the treatment of research expenditure in the former polytechnics. It defied experience and common sense to conclude, as HEFCE did, that the post-1992 universities were well funded by comparison with the old universities, but HEFCE persisted in this view, which still haunts a number of institutions, including London Guildhall.
4   It was later decided to cease all teaching of geography.
5   Although it will be no surprise that there has been a tendency over time for the number to increase.

7

HEARTBREAK ENDING FOR A FOREIGN AFFAIR

David Warner

Introduction

> Swansea Institute of Higher Education is to abandon the battle for
> survival as an independent institution and seek a link-up with the
> University of Wales or the University of Glamorgan.
>
> A working group set up earlier in the year to consider the Insti-
> tute's future has concluded: 'The long-term future of the Institute
> does not lie in preserving its independence'.

This is the headline from *The Times Higher Education Supplement*
of 28 November 1997, which met the eyes of the author just a
few days after he had been interviewed for the post of principal
of Swansea Institute of Higher Education (hereafter SIHE). Although
the working group report referred to did not say precisely what
is claimed, most people concurred with the sentiments set out
in the *THES* article. Not surprisingly, therefore, the author went
to SIHE on a two-year secondment, fully expecting to return to his
post of pro vice-chancellor in Birmingham in the not-too-distant
future.

At the time of writing almost exactly four years after the article was
published, the policy of the SIHE board of governors is to remain
independent, while collaborating fully with neighbouring FHE
institutions. Full-time undergraduate applications to SIHE have risen
by 17 per cent against a background of an overall decline of 7.5 per
cent in Wales. Each year all full-time and part-time student recruitment targets have been met. All student widening participation benchmarks have been exceeded. SIHE has been awarded the highest
possible financial rating by the Higher Education Funding Council for

Wales (HEFCW). SIHE has gained a reputation throughout Wales as a dynamic and innovative institution and, wonder of wonders, was ranked 31st in the UK in the *Guardian*'s composite league table of HEIs published on 22 May 2001.

How has this remarkable turnaround been achieved? Why did SIHE totter towards the edge of the abyss yet recover to find firm ground? The tale is an intriguing one with a hint or two of scandal, but first the scene will be set.

A little history

The constituent colleges of SIHE were all nineteenth-century foundations: the College of Art being established in 1853, the Teaching Training College in 1872 and the Technical College in 1897, although the initial close relationship of the last-named with Swansea Grammar School could support a claim for origins several centuries earlier. During 1976, the three colleges merged to form West Glamorgan Institute of Higher Education, which in 1992, as a result of the relevant Education Act, metamorphosed into Swansea Institute of Higher Education.

The City and County of Swansea boasts two HEIs: SIHE and the University of Wales Swansea. The latter is currently a constituent college of the federal University of Wales, whereas SIHE is not yet a formal member but is an associate college whose first and higher degrees are awarded by the university. The University of Wales Swansea is the larger HEI and is regarded by everyone as the more senior, but paradoxically it is by far the younger (only founded in 1920), having spun out of the Technical College and only coming into separate existence through the chance availability of a greenfield site. Indeed, the promoters of the 'Swansea University College' originally intended it to comprise the Technical College, as the science and technology faculty, and the Teacher Training College as the core of the 'essential' arts faculty (see Dykes 1992: Chapter 3).

Some key facts

Wales has a total population of just under 3 million people yet currently has 13 HEIs.[1] Each aspect of higher education in Wales is, therefore, on a smaller scale than in England and SIHE is by no means the smallest HEI in the principality. The institute's key features include:

- A student population[2] of approximately 5500, of whom 66 per cent are studying full-time and 34 per cent part-time.
- Four per cent of these students are taking FE level courses (primarily foundation art and design) and 14 per cent are on postgraduate or similar professional programmes.
- Forty-nine per cent of these students come from the immediate Swansea Bay area, 67 per cent from South Wales and 77 per cent from Wales.
- In October 1999, 33 per cent of SIHE's full-time undergraduate intake were mature students and of the remaining 'young' undergraduate intake, 98 per cent came from state schools or colleges; 35 per cent came from social classes IIIM, IV and V and 20 per cent came from low-participation neighbourhoods.
- The production of a financial surplus in each of the past six years well in excess of 3 per cent of turnover, which is the main reason for SIHE's good financial rating.

Mission

The above statistics show that SIHE is now operating not only well but in conformity with its long established mission, which states *inter alia*:

> The Institute is a vocational, comprehensive, regionally-based, student-centred institution of higher education, principally serving South Wales, and encouraging national and international access. The specific mission is to support life-long learning by providing high quality and flexible educational opportunities of an applied nature, adding value for its students and staff, the local environment and communities beyond.

The original problems

Until 1992, the Welsh Institutes of Higher Education, including SIHE, were under LEA control and ownership. This meant a low priority for funding for the maintenance of buildings, tight limits on the size of personnel establishments and gradings, and little opportunity to expand home student numbers. In England, the polytechnics and HE colleges had been freed from such LEA control some three years earlier. They were revelling in the last days of Thatcherism: increasing home student numbers as fast as they could, seeking to be entrepreneurial and to diversify and to increase their sources of income, and trying to recruit as many full-cost[3] international students as possible.

It was clear that the then principal of SIHE, Dr Gerald Stockdale, also wanted a share of this action and sought to achieve it in the international arena. However, unlike other HEIs, whose primary tactic was to bring full-cost international students to the UK and teach them on existing courses, SIHE decided to create new franchised[4] courses overseas. As a result, courses, primarily at sub-degree level, were established in several countries, but especially in Malaysia, China, Indonesia and Kenya. The growth of this activity was quite phenomenal. Starting in the late 1980s, by 1995–6 SIHE had 2122 students in South East Asia and Africa at a time when its home student population in Swansea was only 3748. The growth in South East Asia was achieved by creating a partnership, which had not received appropriate approvals, with a Malaysian educator/entrepreneur who not only recruited students for a commission, but also appears to have been heavily involved in the delivery of most of the courses concerned.

It could be argued that Dr Stockdale was a man of some vision and foresight. After all, no less a person than the Prime Minister, Tony Blair, has recently set up an initiative (named after himself) to increase the UK's role in the international student market. Dr Stockdale was there first. Unfortunately, whereas everyone in HE knows about the 'PM's initiative', almost no one, including the generality of staff and members of the board of governors at SIHE, knew about Dr Stockdale's activities.

The full story of the SIHE crisis is documented and published in three reports (NAO 1997; Public Accounts Committee 1997; Welsh Funding Council Audit Service 1997), which tend to be somewhat repetitive. From these reports the major problems may be summarized as follows:

- The SIHE board of governors never approved or even considered the international strategy.
- The establishment and quality arrangements for the international courses were entirely without the normal procedures used for home courses. Indeed, in the case of quality controls, they seem to have been almost non-existent.
- The international activities were never properly costed and consequently it is impossible to determine whether they were operated at a profit or a loss. Other abnormalities in the financial arrangements were also noted.
- There were poor controls over the production and issue of certificates overseas.

- The then principal undertook a large amount of international travel in connection with the unapproved strategy, not all of which, as far as the authors of the reports can see, appear to have been justified (for instance, Dr Stockdale went to Kenya on 18 occasions, involving 21 weeks overseas, incurring travel and subsistence expenses of £24,989 and producing a total income to SIHE of £28,659).

The discovery[5]

The extent of SIHE's involvement overseas gradually became known to more and more staff during the early 1990s, but it was not until February 1995 that the situation became public. A report by SIHE's internal auditors revealed that the then chairman of governors and Dr Stockdale had both visited Malaysia with their wives some 12 months earlier. This report was leaked to the press and HEFCW's audit service undertook an investigation. During the same year there was a little cosmetic internal reorganization (the chairman was not even re-elected to the board of governors) but, of most importance, SIHE's 'application to the Privy Council for degree-awarding powers was rejected because, amongst other things, there were concerns about the quality control arrangements for overseas provision' (NAO 1997: 3).

Staff concern was exacerbated when the principal made a proposal to the board of governors to reorganize SIHE's management and faculty structures and thereby probably make redundant certain staff who had become increasingly critical. On 24 June, votes of no confidence in the principal and vice-principal were passed at a staff meeting and these were subsequently endorsed at a meeting of the academic board. At around the same time, a local Swansea MP, who was also a member of the Committee of Public Accounts, briefed the NAO on the problems that were coming to light and that body prompted HEFCW to prepare the report referred to above.

The SIHE board of governors invited Professor John Andrews, the chief executive of HEFCW, to a special meeting on 15 July. In the light of his comments and those from a meeting of the academic board that followed immediately thereafter, the board of governors asked Dr Stockdale and the vice-principal to resign. Dr Stockdale's letter of resignation arrived the following day, before he had received the formal request. The vice-principal declined to resign and was suspended pending an internal inquiry. As a result of this inquiry, the vice-principal was dismissed, but about 18 months later he was successful in his appeal to an employment tribunal, although he was not reinstated.

Little of this crisis took place behind closed doors. The local and national press were well informed and had a field day, as the following headlines selected from a single 14-day period in July 1996 show:

Storm hits Swansea boss. Front page *THES*, 5 July

Auditors go in to check on college. *South Wales Evening Post*, 9 July

New blow rocks college principal. *South Wales Evening Post*, 12 July

City MP joins college row. *South Wales Evening Post*, 16 July

College head resigns after Commons call. *Daily Telegraph*, 17 July

Heartbreak ending for a foreign affair. Front page, *South Wales Evening Post*, 18 July

A sting in the tale

Even with the resignation of the principal, the sad tale was not over. On incorporation in 1992, the SIHE board of governors had issued Dr Stockdale with a new contract of employment. This provided for the incumbent to receive three years' pay in lieu of notice, plus pension enhancement should SIHE dispense with his services. This would have been valued at £314,000. As it happens, Dr Stockdale resigned, but nevertheless other aspects of his contract were honoured (including pension enhancement), at a cost of £118,921.

Both the three-year period of notice and the acceptance of a resignation from someone who appears to have been responsible for serious mismanagement appear to have greatly annoyed the Public Accounts Committee. As a result, all the contracts of senior staff in Wales were examined and a prohibition was placed on periods of notice exceeding one year. The resignation/dismissal issue is more complicated, especially in the light of the SIHE vice-principal's success at an employment tribunal.

The causes?

The various reports conclude that the problems at SIHE came about for two main reasons. First, there was a blurring between governance and management. The full board of governors was kept in ignorance both by the management and by some senior members of the board, who conspired and contrived to create strategy within an inner cabinet. The board of governors could not therefore exercise proper controls. This situation was facilitated by the fact that the vice-principal was also the clerk to the board of governors. Second, the principal and vice-principal has been in post for almost 20 years, and in the words of the Public Accounts Committee (1997: vi), 'had become possessive of the affairs of the Institute'. In effect, it could be argued that they thought and behaved as if their managerial interests were automatically and entirely synonymous with those of the institute itself.

However, despite everything that had gone wrong, all the reports are unanimous in stating that, 'There is no criticism of the way Swansea-based activities were managed' (NAO 1997: 11). Sadly, few people either within or without Swansea seemed to be aware of this fact.

Continuing problems

As a result of the crisis described above, by September 1996 SIHE was in internal turmoil and lacking in direction. The application for taught degree-awarding powers, which had previously been seen as essential to the institute's future, had been turned down. A considerable number of governors were recently appointed to replace those who had resigned in protest at the situation. The post of principal had been filled in a holding capacity by the remaining assistant principal, who was close to retirement. The vice-principal was still suspended from duty and subject to a painful inquiry, which eventually led to his dismissal, and the institute still had a huge commitment to students overseas.

At this juncture, Mr Roy Phelps, then area manager of the Midland Bank (now HSBC), was appointed chairman of the board of governors. Mr Phelps was a strong, no-nonsense character who had little knowledge or direct experience of higher education, but was determined to hold the institute together. There is no question that at first he succeeded in doing this, but gradually he alienated almost all the staff he had appointed to new senior positions, the acting principal whom he appointed after the holding principal had retired and, in due course, even the author of this case study, whom Mr Phelps was also instrumental in appointing.

Why was this the case? Ironically, it was again because the important distinction between governance and management was not maintained. However, on this occasion the pendulum had swung the other way. Mr Phelps quickly began to regard himself as the *de facto* principal of the institute. He established a permanent office in the senior management suite, he invited staff to call in and see him at will, he excluded the two real principals from key decisions and he used the new clerk to the board of governors, who was again also a member of the senior management team, as his 'man'.

To some it seemed that the cure had become worse than the illness. Staff morale at the institute was at a low ebb. In the view of such external agencies as HEFCW, the institute was in a sorry state and not only was required to report monthly on its activities, but really had no independent future. The other HEIs in Wales kept their distance, with the exception of those that scented a quick kill and the opportunity to pick over the bones. Worst of all, however, given the student recruitment profile of SIHE, its reputation and image locally was in tatters, albeit unfairly. Perhaps, therefore, no one should have been surprised at the extract from the *THES* that introduces this chapter.

With the benefit of hindsight, however, the underlying problem for SIHE was not the international adventures *per se*, but the fact that they had caused the senior managers at the time to take their eyes off the ball. The lure of foreign gold and the consequent disarray meant that the development of the core business back in Swansea had been somewhat ignored. Notwithstanding the constraints, no real attempt was made to try to increase home student numbers. Franchising to FE was minimal and some opportunities were missed in the field of in-service teacher education. One of the most glaring omissions seems to me to be the failure to put in a bid for the various NHS contracts when they became available in the early to mid–1990s. Elsewhere in the UK most of these contracts went to 'modern' universities and SIHE appears to have been well placed, with its strong vocational mission and an existing department of nursing that, although small, is held in high regard locally. If SIHE had gained these contracts, then it would now be almost the same size as the University of Wales Swansea, with the power balance consequently different.

A similar mistake was made in failing to purchase a large, near-derelict site adjacent to SIHE's main campus. The acquisition of this site, which was originally the Swansea Workhouse and more recently a hospital, would have almost doubled the size of the institute's land-locked campus and provided wonderful opportunities for expansion in the future. And at such a low price – rumoured to be just over £100,000.

The overarching problems of Welsh HEIs

The second wave of problems described above ensured that SIHE remained in a parlous state and, to make matters worse, it was an integral part of an HE system that as a whole suffered and, at the time of writing, continues to suffer from a number of overarching problems. The author has written at greater length on these issues in Chapter 8 of *The State of UK Higher Education* (Palfreyman and Warner 2001), but here are the main points:

- Over the past few years the majority of Welsh HEIs have failed to meet their home undergraduate student recruitment and, thereby, population targets.
- The Welsh HEIs are dependent upon 'importing' students from England (and other parts of the European Union) to meet their home student targets. The extent of this dependence is debatable, but it is of interest to note that the two HEIs that are seen by many as being the most 'Welsh' (University of Wales Aberystwyth and Bangor) are those most dependent upon English students.
- Although considerably improved in the December 2001 Research Assessment Exercise, the research record of Welsh HEIs is generally worse than that of their English peers and, certainly, they currently win far fewer grants from the national research councils.
- Historically, the student unit of resource (i.e. the amount of money paid on average for each eligible full-time student recruited) has been lower in Wales than in England and much lower than in Scotland.
- While the income is arguably lower, the costs of providing HE in Wales are probably higher than in most parts of England. The reasons for this are variable, but include: the impact of bilingualism (under the provisions of the Welsh Language Act all public sector organizations are required to produce external publications in both Welsh and English, all signage must be in both languages, initial telephone reception should be in Welsh, provision must be made at all meetings involving the public for simultaneous translation and so on); the costs of maintaining the federal structure of the University of Wales, which some see as good value for money and others do not; the intransigent topography of Wales, which makes it easier to travel from Swansea to most parts of England than, say, to Bangor.
- The fact that Wales is one of the poorest regions of Europe and, as such, a large part of the principality is designated as an Objective One area (i.e. its per capita GDP is less than 80 per cent of the European Union average). This places a disproportionate burden

on Welsh HEIs, which are being required to do more and more to assist their local economies.

* The large number and relatively small size of many Welsh HEIs means that they struggle to meet the increasing bureaucratic and accountability requirements that are now deemed necessary by government of all types to ensure that public funding is used efficiently, effectively and in accordance with their policy imperatives.

Notwithstanding the fact that, *de jure*, the National Assembly for Wales currently has few powers regarding higher education, it is perhaps not overly surprising in the light of the above that one of its first major investigations has been a policy review of Welsh HE (National Assembly for Wales 2002). This review has more than 70 recommendations and does not hesitate to suggest that some HEIs should merge. It does not, however, propose that SIHE should merge, but encourages the University of Wales Swansea and Swansea Institute 'to develop their close working relationship, and to extend collaboration with the local FE colleges' (*ibid.*: 77). Elsewhere, it recommends that SIHE should seek to become a university college (possibly free-standing) via established QAA procedures (*ibid.*). In the next section of this chapter I consider what the future might be for SIHE taking into account the Assembly's views.

The recovery strategy

The first task for the author in January 1998, as the new principal of SIHE, was to evaluate the situation and to make recommendations about the future of the institution. It did not take very long to realize that, as the various reports had indicated, the core business based at Swansea was sound and that all the original problems had either been overseas or had been caused by neglect. The board of governors supported the principal in this assessment and left him to develop the tactics that would move SIHE forward. What were needed were early successes and obvious indicators of change, so that the staff would gain the sweet taste of victory, rather than the bitter one of defeat.

During the first few months, the following key actions were taken. First, the intakes to all international franchised courses were stopped immediately, while ensuring that no student already on-course would suffer in any way. Given the original problems, readers might be surprised to learn that this step had not already been taken, but it had not. SIHE's controlled method of disengagement was subsequently praised by the British Council.

Hitherto, some courses at SIHE had been validated by the University of Wales and some by the University of the West of England. To ensure a greater uniformity of student experience, it was decided to move all validation to a single provider, the University of Wales. Initially, it was intended that this change should be effected over a three-year period on an intake-by-intake basis. However, student demand for change was so great that it was introduced all at once, with every student affected signing an appropriate consent form. A full validation exercise was also successfully undertaken to gain University of Wales awards for SIHE's research degree programme.

Given the time of year, little could be done to increase full-time student applications for the forthcoming academic year. Instead, considerable emphasis was placed on converting those who had already applied into 'bums on seats'. As a result, full-time recruitment was strong and, when coupled with a major part-time campaign that reversed the decline in student numbers in that area, meant that SIHE was full – with home students.

The marketing unit was restructured and strengthened. Challenging performance targets were set, including the production of at least one media release per working day, and, in due course, the unit was relocated for practical and symbolic reasons next to the principal's office.

These initial actions significantly raised staff morale and created fertile conditions for the next stage on the road to recovery, which involved a complex array of approaches that can be summarized as follows.

Creating and maintaining a positive image of SIHE in the minds of the local community, potential customers (which to some extent is one and the same group) and the key decision-makers in Wales. The new approach to marketing was instrumental in achieving this objective, together with the willingness of staff, governors and students 'to talk up the institute'. The principal played his part by putting on weight, i.e. networking as widely and frequently as possible in the region and consequently, in the immortal words of Dr Peter Knight, vice-chancellor of UCE Birmingham, 'having to eat the dinners'.

Meeting all student recruitment targets by both increasing applications and optimizing conversion rates. A deliberate decision was taken to over-recruit in order to maximize widening participation opportunities and to indicate to the Funding Council that SIHE was ready and able to expand. It quickly became obvious that action was also required to improve student retention rates, which, *inter alia*, have a significant impact on recruitment targets.

Examining the existing course portfolio and introducing innovative programmes that both appeal to the customer and develop incrementally from existing expertise. These new courses include animation, music technology, motorsport management, automotive design and what is probably the first undergraduate degree in the world in motorsport engineering. Some courses, particularly in the computing area, were rebadged and a growing portfolio of taught masters courses (including the first in the UK in e-commerce) has been established. A few courses that were not popular have been terminated, but, as in most HEIs, more pruning is almost certainly needed.

Ensuring that a financial surplus of not less than 3 per cent of turnover was produced annually, thereby meeting the Funding Council's criterion of good practice. This target has been achieved by a number of tactics, including: the establishment of a resources group, which allocates staffing and recurrent money to operating units (including faculties) by negotiation informed by benchmark models; increasing the efficiency of the non-core activities such as catering, residences and security; gradually reducing the number of middle level and senior managers in post; and examining every area of activity on a regular basis to eliminate unnecessary practices. The result has been the accumulation of liquid assets that now exceed debt commitments, a reserve from which significant improvements have been made to halls of residence without external borrowing and a 'war chest' to fund opportunistic estate acquisitions and to enable bold steps to be taken in an uncertain future.

Devolving more and more responsibility to faculties, particularly in the area of academic quality. SIHE is a small HEI and, as such, is able to avoid the centre–periphery split that bedevils so many institutions.

Collaborating with other Welsh HEIs, particularly the University of Wales Swansea, and further education colleges in the region when it is mutually advantageous to do so. On the academic side, this collaboration has already resulted in joint courses in public services, performing arts and digital media, the provision of FE-owned courses on SIHE's sites in English language and Welsh and the abolition of tuition fees for SIHE staff taking postgraduate programmes at the University of Wales Swansea. Similar achievements have been secured in other areas such as staff development, the shared usage of playing fields, the publication of a joint student newspaper and procurement.

Improving communications with staff by reintroducing a staff newsletter, frequent usage of the intranet for updating on events and successes, maintaining good relationships with campus trade unions and holding a biannual 'state of the nation' address by the principal to all staff. This last item is an opportunity not only to hear what the principal thinks is likely to happen over the next six months, but also to ask the awkward questions. It has become an example of the new 'openness' that pervades SIHE.

Maintaining a harmonious and balanced working relationship between the senior management and the board of governors. This is due primarily to the appointment of a chairman (George Sambrook) and a deputy chairman (Gareth Roberts) who are instinctively aware of the correct boundary between governance and management. They ensure that the management keeps the board fully informed without appearing to act as the astute 'policemen' they undoubtedly are. Their work has been greatly facilitated by the appointment of a clerk to the board of governors (Clayton Heycock) from outside of SIHE on a part-time basis. Initially, the author was dubious about the possibility of someone who was not actively employed in HE having the skills and cultural background to do this work. The author was completely wrong and is now a strong supporter of this separation of responsibilities. Other procedural changes have also contributed to this situation, such as: the introduction of clear standing orders and a new style of minuting for committees; the preparation of a governors' handbook and training programme; the establishment of an interview-based procedure for the recommendation of the appointment of new governors rather than the previous more informal arrangements; a rolling programme of 'meet the faculty' sessions; and an open invitation to all governors to attend any meeting of the academic board as observers.

Conclusions

The original crisis at SIHE was one of the first to bring to the attention of all the relevant authorities the dangers in trying to run courses overseas as opposed to recruiting international students to home-based programmes. As a result, much tighter controls have been put in place throughout the UK regarding the whole area of collaborative course provision (franchising in particular), academic quality control mechanisms and the costing and pricing of international activities. These changes have done much to bolster the reputation of UK higher education overseas and to provide a sounder platform for the future provision of overseas courses, which is an activity almost certain to continue to grow.

The original crisis also revealed the dangers in allowing independent, albeit substantially publicly funded, organizations to offer their senior managers contracts without any external guidance. Such guidance is now available and the concept of more than one year's period of notice has vanished from HE. The various reports about the crisis also strongly hinted that the tenure of senior managers should in future be limited. It is perhaps not altogether a coincidence, therefore, that a large proportion of new principal/vice-chancellor posts are currently being offered for a fixed period (say, three, five, ten years) with the possibility of renewal.

Finally, the original crisis sowed the seeds for the continuing problems that beset SIHE by allowing the core business at Swansea to stagnate, by building up a negative image in the locality and by creating a leadership vacuum. To their eternal credit, it was the staff at SIHE who finally drew a line in the sand and took on the senior management. But these struggles left them exhausted and they were all too ready to cling to any rock in a storm that seemed to offer survival at whatever cost.

The recovery strategy described above was not, therefore, rocket science. What was needed was a partnership (greatly facilitated by an independent clerk) between a board of governors that provided stability and balance and a new principal who could come from outside of SIHE (and indeed from outside of Wales) and reassure everyone that the institute was doing a good job, that it was worth saving and that it *could* be saved. The adoption of a clear set of targets (particularly to recruit well, to become financially strong and to gain a positive public image) was important, but essentially the strategy was based upon bringing to the surface what was already there and just adding a big dose of confidence: in effect, seeing the glass as half full rather than half empty. Significant change was required, but in order not to be yet another threat, it was achieved slowly and imperceptibly, like the cells of a body, which are replaced regularly while the person appears to remain the same.

Looking through a glass, darkly

The future of SIHE would appear to be set fair. There seems to be no reason why the institute should not retain its independence, continue to recruit well, more than balance its books, gain a good Continuation Audit from the QAA,[6] continue to enhance its reputation within Wales and, overall, meet its mission objectives. In due course, it seems that the other members of the University of Wales would welcome SIHE as a full member, that a limited research profile could be developed and that HEFCW would fund some student expansion, not least to compensate for a recruitment shortfall elsewhere in Wales. This is the final paragraph that I would have written had the National Assembly's Policy Review of Higher Education in Wales not taken place.

The review, however, indicates that the status quo is not an option for the Welsh HE system. In general terms it is highly critical of the federal University of Wales, it is inconsistent regarding the future relationship between FE and HE and it threatens to add planning powers to the current financial role of HEFCW. More specifically, it urges SIHE to collaborate with the University of Wales Swansea and local FE colleges and to seek university college status. To add spice to the pie, the vice-chancellor of the University of Wales Swansea has just announced that he will retire in September 2003. What, then, should the senior managers of SIHE do?

At the time of writing, the institute's tactics are to continue to perform well, while keeping as many options open as possible. Good working relationships have been developed with the University of Wales Lampeter, collaboration with the University of Wales Swansea is thriving, joint programmes have been started with two local FE colleges and the institute is rapidly becoming a strong supporter of the University of Wales, even though it is not yet a member.

To make predictions at this stage is a risky venture, but the author has decided to be bold. I believe that by the end of 2008 there will be a confederation of higher education institutions in South West Wales within the University of Wales. This strong 'cluster' will be well on the way to rationalizing overlapping subject provision, creating new programmes from the synergy achieved, rapidly expanding research and (when the local FE colleges join the confederation) maximizing student progression opportunities. Time will, of course, tell.

Notes

1   The total is 14 if the Open University in Wales is included.
2   The figures are taken from the return to HEFCW in November 2002.
3   The term 'full-cost' describes the tuition fees paid by those international students who come from outside of the European Union to study in the UK and for whom the HEI receives no funding whatsoever from the relevant Funding Council. The level of tuition fee paid by each student is determined by the HEI and usually bears no relation to either market factors or the actual cost of the course taken. 'Full-cost fees' therefore often vary between HEIs and sometimes within them. They are, however, rarely less than £6000 per student per annum (and often much more) and consequently constitute a vital and major source of income to many HEIs.

4   There are numerous different types of relationship between educational organizations. Most of these are described in Palfreyman *et al.* (1998: Chapter 7). Franchising is dealt with in more detail in Palfreyman and Warner (2002: Chapter 17). The essential legal point is that the students concerned always remain students of the franchising institution and not the franchisee.

5   This section is based heavily on the NAO (1997).

6   SIHE's five yearly continuation audit took place at the end of 2001. The report, which is publicly available, is an excellent one.

8

THE LAMBETH HIKE

Adrian Perry

Introduction

College crises can come in many forms. The Lambeth College case study does not show crisis management in the sense of a response to a single cataclysm – a one-off explosion, a public relations disaster or a sudden and unpredictable eventuality – when the recommendation would be to put into effect a carefully crafted continuity plan. Nor was it a financial crisis caused by a swift loss of income or an unpredicted rise in project costs. The study looks instead at how managers and governors responded to the pressing need for a swift change of direction and a step change in quality, cost and flexibility in response to a new and more rigorous climate.

This is not to deny the need that many further education colleges had to manage conventional crises, particularly financial problems, in the incorporated era. At the depths of FE's money problems, in 1996–7, 96 out of 450 colleges were in the lowest financial security category, and providing recovery plans to their Funding Council. This was a consequence of a number of factors.[1] There was certainly some evidence that managerial skills had not kept pace with the challenges of independence, but 'pilot error' cannot be the whole story when a quarter of English colleges are in the same trouble. An overcomplicated funding system had been made more punitive by real terms reductions in the FE budget. The anxieties about colleges at the time were almost entirely financial – and it was not only the system's managers in Coventry who felt this obsession. Budget concerns dominated the sector's internal discourse too. Low funded colleges attacked their better funded colleagues, commercially focused institutions sparred with those with a community ethos and provincial colleges criticized London weightings. Indicators of academic performance had to wait, but the league table of unit costs came out in the first year of the Funding Council's existence.

By the turn of the century, however, the anxieties about college performance had moved to a different field, one of quality. The Minister for Lifelong Learning, Margaret Hodge, gave a lecture (Raising Standards conference 7 March 2002) giving pointers as to how one might start the 'rebuilding of further education'. In a lecture to the RSA, the chair of the Learning and Skills Council, Bryan Sanderson, compared FE colleges to market traders (Sanderson 2001). His chief executive, John Harwood, appeared shortly afterwards on Radio 4 to condemn not just failing colleges but also those that were merely 'satisfactory'. In this context, a study of a college that faced not just short-term financial problems but also a need to raise quality dramatically straddles the concerns of both eras.

Incorporation

Entering the LSC world

When, in April 2001, the government established a Learning and Skills Council (LSC) to integrate the post-16 worlds of adult, work-based further and sixth form education, a new world was brought into being. There were to be new funding systems, new quality assurance and control mechanisms, a new funding methodology and a changed approach to planning and capacity management. Lambeth College in south London was well equipped to enter this world with some confidence. The most recent inspection, in March 2001, had awarded exceptional grades for both the academic and organizational aspects of the college: its management and governance were described as 'outstanding' (FEFC 2001). An academic performance above national benchmarks was remarkable for a college based in Brixton and Vauxhall, recruiting more deprived adult students than any other in England. In November 2001, the Association of Colleges conferred a Beacon Award for the college's work in the community, and the local Learning and Skills Council recommended it as a construction Centre of Vocational Excellence. Academic success was matched with business strength: the college had built a financial position that not only maintained the grade A rating denied to most FE colleges, but also provided a war chest for ambitious developments in both vocational and sixth-form studies.

The picture at incorporation

The picture painted above showed a marked difference from the college that had to face up to the previous FE sea-change at incorporation. In April 1992, all FE and sixth-form colleges in England were taken out of local authority control and made into independent bodies. John Major hosted a cheer-leading conference in the Queen Elizabeth Conference Centre in Westminster, asking the assembled principals and chairs, 'isn't it great to be free?'. The truth for many colleges was somewhat different. They were about as free as a farmer selling tomatoes to Tesco, or a Marks and Spencer shirt supplier: for the incorporated world was led and organized by a single Further Education Funding Council (FEFC), which soon made clear the austere journey of quality and cost that would need to be travelled by the motley flotilla that was heading out of the local government harbour.

Lambeth in 1992: the background

A forced merger

Lambeth College was particularly poorly prepared for the new world. It had been formed in May 1992 by a shotgun marriage of three former colleges: Brixton College, Vauxhall College and South London College. The local authority had come to the view that these colleges would struggle to survive in an independent world, and needed to be brought together to stand a chance of success. They were not alone: the *Times Educational Supplement* also wondered aloud whether 'the Lambeth three' could survive. This is not to say that all was bleak: all three institutions brought strengths to the table. Brixton College had approached work with disadvantaged adults with flair and invention. Vauxhall College had maintained a broad offer in construction, and had diversified intelligently into business and commercial work. South London maintained some excellent science provision. The staff of all three institutions shared a genuine commitment to widening participation and equal opportunity. But the danger signs were very clear. The crisis that had to be faced had a number of features:

- high levels of unit cost;
- a poor local reputation;
- declining student numbers;
- a staff-centred culture that gave trade unions a veto on innovation;
- low quality in many programmes.

Quality issues

Educationalists have looked at quality in two quite different ways. The input definition used to hold sway: a college was of high quality if it had modern equipment, well stocked libraries, clean and bright classrooms, generous levels of student support, small classes and high volumes of teaching time. However, in recent years and under the prompting of stakeholders in the department and its client agencies – FEFC, inspectorates, HEFC, TECs, now the LSC – an output definition has become dominant. A college shows high quality if it delivers – that word again – above average retention and pass rates, reports strong customer satisfaction and achieves exceptional progression to jobs and higher education.

The Lambeth College that entered incorporation in 1992 struggled in terms of both definitions. The college estate was neglected, with outdated capital equipment. One of the first indications was the threat by a leading examining board to withdraw accreditation for computing courses because of the vintage of the equipment. Results were poor: student dropout was more than one-third, and pass rates were generally below 50 per cent. To take just one example, the A-level pass rate in 1992 was 22 per cent. This contributed to a problematic local reputation, which affected recruitment. The disadvantaged nature of the college student cohort – with the bulk studying at level 2 and below, and more than 80 per cent qualifying for widening participation premiums – provided a ready excuse for poor performance.

Cost problems

Whatever the cause of the quality problems, it wasn't resources: Lambeth was actually well funded. Preliminary investigations (FEFC 1993) suggested it had unit costs 37 per cent above the sector median. This was due to the differences of resource levels under local government. Prior to 1993, local authorities had used a range of schemes of delegation, and exhibited widely differing levels of generosity. Now, the move to a national scheme would involve a move to a national unit cost. This implied that the college would have to find cuts of £8 million or so on a £21 million budget, and in pretty quick order.

Corporate culture

It had been difficult for previous managers to come to terms with their problems of cost and quality because of a combination of circumstances. A decision had been made that former ILEA colleges should delay their entry into the 1988 Education Reform Act's system of local management of colleges, as they were still coping with moving to local borough ownership. This was not a kindness, leaving local managers without the experience of independent decision-making, budgetary autonomy or secure internal information systems. Lambeth's financial controls were sufficiently poor for the FEFC's new chief executive to call the chair and principal to a meeting in Coventry to explain the steps they were taking to improve matters: it was for this reason that the college was granted only provisional incorporation, and was formally the last of England's colleges to enter the world of independence.

A particular local feature was the power of trade unions. Their influence on what was still a very old Labour council was considerable: evidence of problems could be diverted with complaints about 'lack of resources', and managers' attempts to apply financial responsibility resisted by campaigns against the 'cuts'. Union officials were often closer to council decisions than college managers, who sometimes learned second hand about financial cuts or policy switches. When the new principal arrived in June 1992, all teaching staff were on strike and the budget was apparently £1.3 million in the red.[2] He was soon to be briefed by the district HMI in these terms:

- Management clearly unsatisfactory in the past ... Some problem areas in teaching ... Tutorial system generally unsatisfactory
- Space utilisation needs addressing by rationalisation of sites
- On finance – need to get a grip of unit costs and overheads ... Learning resources patchy ... IT stock inadequate ... value for money not good
- Can curriculum quality stand up to competition? Former colleges did not face the issue ... too many staff unaware of world they are now in ... need to rationalise some areas
- Examination results sobering ... tone of complacency and excuses needs to be removed and pass rates and retention raised ... need for an ethos of quality totally absent from previous colleges

Overall there are two major tasks:

- raise your quality considerably;
- radically improve the public perception of the College.

Facing the future: first steps   ■

Sharing the view

There is an anecdote – probably apocryphal – about the education minister of a newly independent Balkan state who said 'I have two problems – one big, and one small. The small problem is that the whole system needs to be changed. The big problem is that no one else can see that.' The first job, then, was to develop among all stakeholders a common understanding of the length of the journey ahead. This was helped by the creation of a new governing body, which shared a perception of the need to change quality and cost, under a powerful and experienced chair, Lorna Boreland Kelly. But staff needed to be brought aboard. An approach based on condemnation was plainly unlikely to succeed, not least because many of the problems had been generated by managerial structures that were none of their doing. What was needed was to build a common approach, based on either shared values ('We all want to reduce student dropout – how can we do it together?') or a realistic understanding of external imperatives ('Of course we'd like a bigger budget – but as that isn't going to happen, what do we do?'). The principal held sessions at each site explaining the new funding demands, going through the performance indicators and inspection systems that were to be introduced nationally, and what this meant for the institution. Communication was strengthened with the introduction of a fortnightly college bulletin, regular cascade sessions and, as appropriate, staff meetings on a centre basis. This emphasis on communication was a persistent theme: later the college successfully adopted Investor in People status, and, to assess the effectiveness of communication and strength of morale against benchmarks, joined the LSDA staff survey pilot.

Using outsiders

In order to develop the shared understanding of the size and urgency of the task, external benchmarks and researchers were used. The college was one of the first to engage in an investigation of retention issues. Dropout rates were universally attributed to the levels of deprivation of the student cohort. Funds were obtained from the local training and enterprise council (TEC) to pay for a study by the Further Education Staff College. The report was written by Paul Martinez (1994), who has since become the guru of retention studies. He compared classes with similar intakes, showing that dropout was not inevitable. Some staff were successful in attracting and retaining students with the most profound personal difficulties. Following up withdrawn students, he discovered that the social factors that had been politely given to tutors as the reason for leaving did not present the whole story. Of course, personal and social difficulties played a part, but academic matters and, especially, weaknesses in tutorial care and guidance also proved to play a major role.

> [The] present research supports other research findings to the effect that, while financial hardship may be an important factor, it is by no means the sole or main determinant of drop-out, and, in the light of the survey data, is unlikely to cause substantial non-completion except in conjunction with other factors.

> If one word arises out of this report with a message for the College it is 'help'. Over and again the factors discriminating between current and withdrawn students point to 'help with course work', 'help in getting a job', 'help with personal problems', 'helpful teachers', 'help in getting qualifications', 'help with career'. In all of these areas, withdrawn students perceive the College more negatively than current students.

The report was disseminated across the college by senior managers, engaging staff in a debate about how the college course offer and student service systems might be better adapted to meet the needs of students. The slide that contrasted essentially similar NVQ2 construction programmes that differed wildly in student success was pointedly titled 'the heroes and the zeroes'.

Similar use of critical friends was employed to spark a debate about costs and efficiency. In order to challenge the view that the college's problems were a simple product of its environment, colleagues from colleges with lower costs but similar missions came to the college: George Sweeney (later Sir George) talked to governors about how his college – serving tough estates on Merseyside – could produce exceptional results within acceptable levels of cost. The appointment of an exceptional finance director from outside the college was another crucial step forward.

Convergence

Beefing up the finance function did not occur a moment too soon. A complex unit-based funding system was adopted by the FEFC, paying for each student place by calculating how many units it earned. A short course was worth fewer units than an all-year programme; expensive programmes like craft construction drew down more units than cheaper classes in humanities or business studies. This unitized system enabled easy comparison between the costs of various colleges, even those with different missions or course profiles. As feared, the FEFC confirmed a policy of 'convergence' – migrating all college costs to a single national level.[3] The college entered the incorporated world with a unit funding level of £30.92, compared with a target of £18.50.[4] The college was helped by the FEFC's decision to phase this move over a number of years. The journey would plainly need cuts, but there was equally plainly some fat on the beast at the start.

The fact that swift action on cost saving could – in the window before full convergence hit – be used to generate investment funds helped to garner support for more efficient practices. Economies freed up resources to improve areas that had long frustrated staff. When the first major move was made to improve staff utilization – teachers had generally been deployed four hours a week below their contracted contact time – the savings would be used as a one-off sum to modernize computer stock. Similarly, the evacuation and sale of sites as the college adopted more effective space utilization made available disposal receipts that could modernize and maintain the remaining estate. Crèches were built, study centres created, access funds and fee remission increased. The message was clear: if we can act sensibly, we can focus our budget on the areas of real need.

Governors considered whether to move to the new national level in a short sharp campaign, or to move down over a longer period. The decision was taken to choose a 'soft landing', not least in the hope of a return of a Labour government that would moderate the reduction in the unit of resource. Electoral rescue did not happen, but this decision nevertheless proved to be the right one. It is doubtful whether taking out 200 staff and seven sites in a single round was practicable, even if the damage to public perception or the industrial relations consequences could have been handled. However, the practice of extending the agony had its disadvantages, as it required a sustained series of cuts and redundancies over a period of five years, damaging staff morale and diverting management attention away from the quality agenda. There was also a danger that, after a few tough decisions, a determination to drive through the unpleasant aspects of the financial recovery plans might be softened, placing the college back in peril. The momentum of cost reduction was maintained by adopting an austere financial goal – governors instructed managers that the college should always be in financial category A, requiring action that maintained adequate reserves and cash flow.

Going for growth

Another important decision was taken: to try to grow the student numbers coming to the college. This was based upon two motives:

• A social drive to raise qualifications and skills in local people. Lambeth shared the same skills profile as much of London: many more graduates (often incomers) and many more totally unqualified people than national averages. An effective college could make a great contribution in bridging the gap between wards that had unemployment rates twice the national average, and a buoyant economy eager for skilled workers.
• A financial driver, in that additional students could moderate the effects of financial convergence on the budget. The demand on managers would therefore be to increase provision within a static budget, by more efficient resource utilization, rather than maintain numbers against a declining resource base.

The problem was where to generate the growth from. Reputation – and long established travel-to-study patterns – made it difficult to attract substantial numbers of able 16-year-olds. Expanding provision for the employed was difficult when two-thirds of local people travelled to work outside the borough. However, there was substantial evidence of local demand for community and vocational studies at a lower level than the former colleges had provided. One of the constituent colleges, for example, had provided no engineering courses below National Diploma – this in a borough where only one-quarter of school leavers were qualified to enter at that level. Reform of the course portfolio to create provision more closely aligned to local demand generated growth. In 1994–5, the college's first FEFC unit target of 623,000 units was exceeded by nearly 9 per cent.

The college's desire to build growth was helped by a decision, taken by the local authority after partnership discussions with the college, to absorb the work of the LEA community education service. This was expansion by acquisition rather than organic growth, but it opened new opportunities for progressions as local people in community centres – the college is currently delivering on 30 or more sites – could progress to mainstream courses at the major centres. Further growth was bought via franchise – not the distant commercial partners that troubled the government, but outreach to local community-based charitable trainers. The attitude was one of 'partners not punters': the college contracted at generous rates, and worked with its partners to ensure they were able to meet funding agency quality and information demands. By 2001, the college unit total was exceeding 1,100,000.

Marketing

The decision to go for growth by a revised course offer and community partnership rather than a major advertising campaign reflected a mature understanding by governors and senior managers about the nature of marketing. Marketing activities involve identifying the particular wants and needs of a target market of customers, and then going about satisfying those customers – if possible, better than the competition. Marketing is not simply promotion. However, college employees have in the past sometimes felt that the function of marketing is to supply the type of students they would like to teach to the courses they would like to teach. Thus, any shortfall in course numbers is attributed to poor marketing, as evidenced by the lack of sufficient course leaflets, radio advertisements or glossy prospectuses. Within the senior discussions of the college, there was an understanding that launching a major promotional campaign before the product was right would be unsuccessful, and might actually work to impede longer-term efforts to raise the reputation and enrolments of the college. The one new image that was suggested – to change the name of the college to the College of South London – was vetoed in 1992 by a governing body containing a substantial number of LEA nominees. The name 'Lambeth' is still a marketing drawback, enduringly associated with the performance and quality levels delivered by the difficult and chaotic local authority of the 1980s.

Sharing success

Quality revisited

The college had now to turn to improving its retention and achievement figures. This would be essential to sustaining the growth and thus financial security of the college, but it was first and foremost an educational imperative. So many of the college's students were coming back to education from an unsuccessful school experience: to fail them again was particularly disappointing.

A first step was to get believable figures: what was really happening out in the classrooms and laboratories? This required much more effective performance of the management information function, which was remodelled as 'college information services' or CIS, to show that good information flows benefited the entire organization, not just the bosses. Effective leadership of the team was brought in, and supported: whatever they said was taken to be the truth unless disproved. The litany common in failing institutions – 'Candidly, Principal, I believe my figures rather than yours . . . these statistics don't smell right' – was heard less and less. By 2001, inspectors were able to comment that 'teachers and managers have confidence in data relating to courses and student performance'.

Getting the right information was an important first step. Managers learned one of the hardest tales of college recovery, that when you find the truth it is often dispiriting.[5] Areas that had been felt to be satisfactory, teams felt to be reliable, were not. The first authentic series of figures revealed the college's retention to be around 65 per cent, its achievement probably less than 50 per cent. There were still areas where good information was difficult to secure, and 'dipstick' checks were used to give managers some grasp of levels of, for example, attendance and room utilization. Slowly, a comprehensive suite of believable numbers emerged.

Knowing where you are is a good start to any journey, but it is only a start. If the college had been content with merely collecting figures rather than improving them it would have been vulnerable to the FE cliché that 'you don't fatten the pig by weighing it'. An improvement programme was needed, and improvements in quality are rarely swiftly achieved. For every dramatic account of a school or hospital being 'turned around' there is a matching case of improvement by sustained effort through time.

Putting systems in place

Quality systems therefore had to be developed and implemented, with governors establishing targets for improvement in academic and financial areas long before these were to become first fashionable and later obligatory. Course audits fed into the college self-assessment report. Student perception surveys – resisted at first by trade unions who told governors they were 'typical of the college's hectoring and bullying management style' – were used to inform policy and investment. An annual senior management review of results – colloquially known as the Star Chamber – trawled through every one of the thousand or more courses in the college to discover and spread good practice, to praise achievement and to eliminate weakness. Teacher observation was instituted to support evidence-based appraisal of lecturing staff. The effect was to raise the pass rate from 48 per cent in 1996 to 74 per cent by 2000, and to almost halve student wastage in the same period, from 35 to 19 per cent. As a consequence, overall success rates – the expectation of finishing and getting a qualification that a student might reasonably have on entering a programme – therefore rose from 31 to 59 per cent, meaning that, over the college, several thousand more students each year were gaining the certification they needed for higher education or the job market.

The national scene

A level playing field?

By the mid-1990s, there were the first signs that the college was beginning to tackle its problems. Results were creeping up, and the first few rounds of redundancy and premises disposals had been accomplished. However, the financial outlook was still problematical. As we have seen, the national funding system demanded that all colleges conform to the same level of cost. It was plain that, were this policy to be driven through to its finality, even a well managed urban college would suffer increasingly severe problems. Key governors agreed with the principal's view that the funding system gave insufficient weight to two factors:

1 The costs of operating in London. Effectively, the highest London weighting for a college was between 6 and 8 per cent. This reflected the fact that the FEFC refunded the college for the cost of the staff London weighting allowances, but no more. This meant that the higher cost of administrative staff necessary to compete with other London employers, the higher gradings of teaching staff (needed to persuade teachers to stay in the capital) and the greater cost of bought-in services were underrepresented.
2 The additional budgetary demands arising from a disadvantaged student cohort. The original FEFC funding system – unlike the local government systems it replaced – had few concessions for urban disadvantage. Indeed, one can argue that its heavy penalties for low retention were a positive disincentive for the urban college to work with difficult-to-reach groups.

The college maintained its view that deprivation was no catch-all excuse for poor results or high costs, but was reluctant to go to the opposite extreme, that social factors do not matter at all. It was clear that the future success for the college would depend crucially on securing adjustments to funding that treated London costs more realistically, and made appropriate recognition of the challenges of working in a deprived environment. The chair and principal agreed that the time was right to make the case publicly, and engage in lobbying activity via local MPs, the FEFC and the Association of Colleges. This campaigning stance had a secondary benefit, as college staff realized that their concerns were shared by college leaders willing to go out on a limb to fight their cause.

The campaign for London

Lambeth was not the only college to come to these views. The London group of the Association of Colleges commissioned consultants to look at the issue of London costs, and provide a report that could be used to alert the FEFC to the issues. A group of London principals also appeared before a select committee of the House of Commons to argue the capital's case. They were met by a group of MPs, only one of whom came from London, and received an appropriately frosty response. Nevertheless, the evidence became increasingly difficult to resist. The submission to the select committee and the LSE report strongly supported the view that London costs were not met by the existing methodology and provided ammunition that led to the establishment of a special committee of the FEFC, which recommended a higher level of weighting for working in the capital. Lambeth College moved from having a 6 per cent uplift to an 18 per cent uplift. Given the degree of reduction in unit cost required by the process of convergence, this moderated the college programme of cuts rather than created additional income. It was, however, enormously useful in cushioning the financial shocks.

The Kennedy Committee

The issue of deprivation came to be addressed in a different manner. The FEFC established a committee under Helena Kennedy QC (later Baroness Kennedy) to see how further education colleges might widen participation in education. The costs of such work, and the threats to established colleges with a community mission, became apparent. One of the conclusions of the Kennedy Report (1997) was that funding premiums should be made available for work with disadvantaged groups. The criterion was student post code, with additional funding units being available for those coming from addresses within the government's definition of 'worst wards'. This provided an additional damping to the work of convergence, increasing college unit earnings by about 6 per cent.

Lambeth College was prominent in both the London Costs campaign – its principal being on the FEFC London costs committee and appearing before the Select Committee on Education and Employment (28 February 1998) – and the Kennedy debate – presenting evidence on behalf of the urban colleges in membership of the Association of Colleges. The effort had played a part in securing a very substantial benefit to the college, effectively raising the funded average level of funding (ALF) by 18 per cent. The campaign was plainly worthwhile, but the benefit was weakened when national factors caused the target ALF to drop 7 per cent from £18.50 per unit to £17.20.

Financial progress

The remorseless progress to the target ALF continued through the 1990s, moderated as we have seen by the effects of a more favourable London weighting and by the recommendations of the Kennedy Committee. The college's funded ALF fell from £30.92 in 1993–4 to £17.22 in 2001–2. We have noted that this fall was moderated; on the other side, however, it must be remembered that no allowance was made for inflation during this period. Taking all factors into account, unit cost fell by 41 per cent over the period, and the improved student success rates meant that value for money – in terms of the cost of a successful completion – must have risen considerably faster.

The moral

The Lambeth case study shows undramatic but consistent recovery from what must in anyone's language be a crisis situation. Tolstoy famously wrote in *Anna Karenina* that all happy families are alike, but each unhappy family is unhappy in its own way. Perhaps unsuccessful colleges are different in their own way, too, but a number of common features would be shared with the Lambeth College of the early 1990s:

- lack of financial information, and little control of costs;
- an overemphasis on the needs of staff and insufficient regard for the needs of the local community and the success of students;
- managers and governors unable to control and direct the path of the institution.

It may be easier to say what was not behind the problems. Working in a deprived area did not seem to be a great factor, though it made it difficult to achieve the consistently high achievement and retention figures needed for 'beacon college' status. Did money matter? Well, any decent public service needs to be well resourced, but the level of cost at the end of the period we have studied was decisively lower than at the beginning. College structures mattered little – a fuzzy matrix was demolished at the beginning to establish clear lines of responsibility but after that the college moved from faculty to school-based academic management, from local to whole college to centre-based delivery of student services, while delivering consistent service improvement.

Nor were the improvements delivered by a transformational incoming management team. While the principal and finance director appointments did come from outside, many of the other important posts were filled internally. In some areas – management information and students with learning difficulties – internal candidates actually took over and improved services that had failed under specially recruited outside 'experts'. Perhaps the moral there is that many employees are eager to do a good job, and can do so once clear purpose and secure information have been established. People were at the core of the improvements, and those with a passion for getting things right were freed to succeed. This meant that those who were not performing had to be removed; at stages in its history the college parted company with a finance director, a human resources director and a curriculum vice-principal.

Questionnaires on management culture suggest that the college blends a pace-setting culture with authoritative (but not authoritarian) style. There is no one style that is a sure guarantee of success, but these do seem appropriate for recovery: a determined identification of the task ahead, and a willingness to roll up sleeves and get it done.

Conclusion

No college is perfect, and Lambeth still has some enduring problems. Retention of students on long courses has improved but is still just around the benchmark for deprived colleges – an uncomfortable position for a college with ambitions to excellence. The adoption of the community education contract has drawn college managers into an awkward position with a local education authority unclear as to whether its relationship with the college is one of purchaser or partner.

There remains a major image problem. Problem reputations endure for long times, even if – as with Skoda cars – the product has changed beyond recognition. Students still leave the borough at 11 and at 16, often to institutions with poorer results and worse inspection reports than Lambeth's schools and college now deliver. The governing body took marketing as a major theme of its 2002 residential conference, aiming to consider how it might help the college to manage its reputation better.

Nor can any college feel it is eternally safe from financial difficulty. The world of further education retains its budget problems. The substantial amount of new money brought in under the 1997 and 2001 Labour governments has been slow to seep through to the college chalk-face. Colleges remain funded at a lower level than schools, and 2002–3 provided the first opportunity in a decade to be funded at a level above inflation. Even this easement was bought at a price, biting into funds available for growth. Local LSCs that had enthusiastically endorsed growth plans of 15 per cent and more found themselves trying to reconcile them with growth funding of around 1 per cent. Any funding methodology will include elements alongside payment for student volumes – fee remission, widening participation, additional learning support – that are policy sensitive, and will affect colleges differentially.

Finally, there is the threat of success – of believing one's own publicity. A college that secures a £1 million surplus and grade 1 in management and governance, that delivers national prizes and teaching grades well above national averages, can nervously feel it has only one way to go. College managers sought a way to push on to excellence, adopting the European Excellence model early in 2002.

Could the college get into trouble again? Of course it could – the educational management world is a tricky place, even if many of the hazards are created by policy makers. Colleges that have coped with the collapse of apprenticeship, the coming of IT, the feminization of the workforce and the reconstruction of traditional industry have been tripped up by franchise regulations, convergence, individual student records and individual learning accounts. The fad for risk management is unlikely to create greater stability, as it seldom predicts the destabilizers that come out of a blue sky. Lambeth College, for example, had £5 million invested in the Allied Irish Bank when that bank was revealed to be damaged by a rogue trader in a minor branch in the USA. How many colleges have the wobble of a major financial institution in their risk assessment?

Yet there is great potential and promise. Lambeth College can feel it is now swimming with the policy tide. The aim to bring help on basic skills to 700,000 adults will require the expertise and reach of a strong urban further education sector. Getting 50 per cent of our young population to university will require the outreach experience of adult and community education. Providing workforce development is an opportunity for colleges who have vocational roots. The Lambeth journey continues, but with a strength, vigour and confidence based on success in a difficult task.

Notes

1 A good survey of successful management of colleges in financial difficulty is to be found in Atkinson (2002).
2 I know this to be true: in the words of the song, 'I was that soldier'.
3 With the exception of London weighting.
4 This 'target ALF' fell to £16.50 at one stage but was £17.20 when achieved in the 2000–1 financial year.
5 Although sometimes not. Many of the colleges 'named and shamed' for their poor academic performance in the mid and late 1990s were in fact suffering from poor data collection. Some principals asked why they should allocate management resources to collecting additional achievement evidence when it had no financial payback.

9

CRISIS MAKING AND CRISIS MANAGING
Chris Duke

Nice day for a crisis, but what do we mean by it?

This chapter offers a comparative and somewhat contrasting perspective for looking at managing crises in universities. It is based on experience of university management in Australian and New Zealand universities as well as in England. It follows the pattern of earlier chapters in adopting a case study approach, and it links this particular story to the literature of crisis, before considering specific issues pertaining to mass higher education systems in crisis more generally.

The chapter differs from others in a somewhat more radical way as well. It shows that crisis may well be manufactured and sustained as a way of exercising a managerial prerogative. Managing crisis here carries the sense of making and using rather than dealing with crises. Rather than mobilizing and leading the creative energies of the institution – what we often call empowerment – it may then be a means of subjugating, and exercising needless control.

Before we look at the particular institutional story, let us ask what we mean by a crisis to be managed. Where does it come from, how serious is it, when is it solved and gone? What is its aftermath and legacy? To what extent is it institutionally unique and what patterns become evident? Is it institutionally unique: a university bankrupt, a chief executive resigned in disgrace, massive underrecruitment, a horrendous legal case overhanging? Or it is systemic and continuing: chronic grinding penury that seems to threaten the very identity of the university and the life of scholarship? Or could it be both, or is it something else again?

There are crises and crises. In the early twenty-first century, branded at this early point the century of globalization, when we have an apparent convergence of systems, problems and solutions around the world, it can be said that a crisis in higher education is universal. In the words of the Edwardian music hall song, 'It's the same the whole world over.' More to the point, the second chorus line may be equally generalizable: 'It's the poor what gets the blame.' If there is a crisis, tighten up, press down, increase control – tough management for tough times.

We have heard and read much about crisis for a couple of decades and more: the crisis in higher education, the crisis of the university, the crisis in the humanities. If crisis is universal, what does it mean to say 'managing crisis'? Why not 'managing normality'? There is a parallel with 'managing change'. We learn that all management is now change management, since change is the only constant; the only certainty is uncertainty. If all management is change management in a system and institutions undergoing continuous change and in continuous crisis, does managing crisis dissolve in our hands? What is special about it?

A framework for looking at crises

We return to the meaning of crisis after looking at the story of one institution. Let us first ask who defines a particular set of circumstances as a crisis. What is the intent and effect of talking and behaving in this way? Why is it a crisis and where does it come from? Does the idea of such a crisis acquire an identity and a life of its own? Whose needs does it serve? Is it protracted and amplified, or defused and dealt with? Is it fact or artefact?

There is nothing new about manufacturing crisis to suit political purpose. The Reichstag burned in the 1930s. Henry IV was credited by Shakespeare with busying giddy minds with foreign quarrels a lot earlier. Mrs Thatcher had a nice home and away crisis – the miners and the Falklands – that served her famously well. John Howard in Australia more recently enjoyed the fruits of joining a war in Afghanistan and having a Tampa refugee crisis in a timely way for the November 2001 election. Universities are political systems as surely as they are educational institutions. Quite a lot about managing crisis may be about understanding when and why it is handy to have one.

Some other prompts may help you to read this particular story thoughtfully and critically. They may also help when looking at other events in your own experience, whether or not labelled crisis or critical, so as to 'read' them from different perspectives.

There is a familiar trilogy of considerations to do with management and organizational behaviour and applied to higher education by Becher and Kogan (1992) in particular: process, structure and culture. Think about their relevance to managing crisis. A starting proposition might be that real crisis demands decisive action, which can be called dramatic process; and that process (or decisive action) may dominate the early hours and days of crisis management. Was 'process' – or particular action – also the precipitating factor, whether the crisis was internally or externally induced?

As the immediacy of crisis recedes and is contained, process remains important, but perhaps the instinct is then to move to a change of structure to prevent repetition and equip the institution to operate differently and more safely. Is crisis managed in the second phase by processes, which lead to new structures, allowing that most restructurings are probably by new institutional heads these days, as an expected energetic honeymoon act?

Does cultural change kick in early, late or not at all? Institutional culture is less tangible and visible than either structure or processes (procedures). Is it seen as central to crisis resolution and longer-term prevention? How long does it take to have an effect in this and more productive senses? Finally, do process (and structural) changes perhaps sometimes serve as a flight from cultural change, tinkering on the surface while the deeper causes of crisis persist and even grow, bringing on new crises before very long?

An instinct when things get difficult is to work harder, and take tighter control to prevent more problems. This is a natural instinct and a wise immediate response, but its useful half-life is short. It leads into (perhaps back into) self-defeating micro-management. Then local experts down the line in more humble specialized areas get over-ridden by less well informed senior managers. Local *tacit knowledge* and *know-how* is brushed aside, along with the significant experience and creative suggestions of those most well informed. Taking command in this way soon creates a raft of new problems and ultimately a new crisis. There is a large difference between addressing the devil in the detail, thus intervening selectively to signal the importance of detail, and undermining those who know best what works at this level.

Finally, in this pre-case study briefing, note the balance between central control and local invigorating energy. Burton Clark captures this in his 1998 study, which teases out among five key dimensions of entrepreneurial capability not just a strong steering core and a diversified income base, but also a reinvigorated academic heartland and an integrated culture and shared purpose. His summative framework is relevant for interrogating the causes of and responses to crisis, short and longer term.

The University of Western Sydney and the mother of restructurings

A very special Australian 'new university'

Space demands that a complicated story be simply told.[1] The University of Western Sydney (UWS) was formed following Australia's 'Dawkins reform' of higher education in the late 1980s. This effectively vetoed very small size institutions. It removed the binary divide, and led to a unified national system (UNS) of some 38 universities, many of them large by British standards. In the process of mergers and take-overs the colleges of advanced education (CAE) were removed from the Australian landscape. Three federated university systems emerged, all in New South Wales. One quickly disaggregated to become (again) the University of New England (UNE) and a new Southern Cross University. A second, Charles Sturt University, quickly integrated its three inherited CAEs with a determinedly unitarist structure.

Both of these federated systems suffered problems of great distance in rural New South Wales. The third federated university system, UWS, was unique, and with unique importance and potential.[2] It is concentrated within the fast growing but socio-economically disadvantaged Greater Western Sydney (GWS) region, which houses some 10 per cent of the whole Australian population. Its three constituent CAEs became members in the UWS federated system, each with two campuses.[3]

The university grew rapidly through the 1990s on the basis of its huge local natural catchment area. UWS became very important to its region, something special, which really belonged to them. Its presence steadily raised the aspirations of the displaced, socially marginalized and ethnically diverse communities – the 'Westies' – that characterize the region. The very low GWS participation in higher education started to climb, both by enrolment in UWS and as rising numbers also enrolled into the several older central or CBD located Sydney universities.[4]

Rumour had it that the three member chief executive officers (CEOs) had a private understanding that they would disaffiliate at some agreed future time when the rapid growth made them each large enough to stand as singular institutions in the UNS. Meanwhile, the university's profile rose rapidly as an object of pride and affection of GWS, long without its own university. By 1997 it was the sixth largest university in the land.[5]

A real crisis and its resolution: 1995

In 1995, soon after the first vice-chancellor was succeeded[6] by a new incumbent, the CEO of UWS Nepean, Jillian Maling, made a disastrous if finely balanced error of judgement. She sought to take Nepean out of the federation and was narrowly defeated in an affair that was both cloak-and-dagger and front-page Sydney media news. She resigned. A part-time administrator was brought in to police the miscreant member, which was temporarily run directly by the UWS vice-chancellor until a new dean, recently appointed from outside, was made acting CEO. A new substantive externally recruited CEO took up office in September 1996, with the task of bringing Nepean back into productive synergy with the rest of UWS, and picking up the threads of rapid and ambitious growth woven together by Maling.

In 1995 a real crisis demanded action. The first stage was to exercise decisive, some would say ruthless, control. Tight close initial management subdued the rebellion and saw off the rumbling opposition and threat of legal actions that followed the initial counter-coup. There followed a protracted interim cooling off period, a holding operation while things settled down and the new CEO was found. During the year that passed, the initial crisis receded but the simmering discontent remained. The centrifugal tendencies that had threatened the federation were replicated at the next level down, led by several faculty deans within Nepean.

The second phase of crisis resolution, and then rebuilding, followed. This was essentially cultural, took 12 months to complete and was structurally expressed. Culture change was the central element and intent, with different, participatory processes as the means, and a 'restructure' giving form to the 'new Nepean' as the tangible initial outcome. The second outcome was markedly increased productivity across all key performance indicators.

The old Nepean symbol of the phoenix was exploited and informally celebrated in collaborative ways. Nepean was seen to have risen anew. Early drafts for changes grew into an agreed and quite different form as a result of diverse input through working parties, *ad hoc* forums and debates at academic board. The process was empowering, the consultation demonstrably authentic. The whole process was completed in less than a year and the new system bedded down fast for the new (1998) year.

A high-risk but important event was a celebratory function to call back and honour the (very remarkable) achievements of the disgraced and resigned former CEO, who had understandably left without acknowledgement much less ceremony. This healed some of the still open wounds from the traumatic mid-1995 crisis and symbolically tied together Nepean's past with its future, rather than leave a gaping rent between. The former CEO's condition for returning for the event was that the chancellor, vice-chancellor and other UWS trustees not be present. The risk was high, but worth taking. Nepean had by then barely won back its credibility and the new CEO (now president) his *bona fides* with trustees.

By the end of 1997 Nepean was in new wind and new shape. The eight former faculties, which had served as administrative and business silos containing nearly 40 departments, were replaced by 20 schools in a 'delayered' flatter structure. These schools, which were self-creating in that all academic staff were required to choose and negotiate their own grouping, affiliations, shared identity and leadership via school chairs, quickly came to work in creative and collaborative competition, networking strongly within as well as beyond the university. They were strongly outward-focused, driven by a wish to perform strongly, and supported through a resource allocation system co-created and owned by the schools themselves.[7]

UWS Nepean made itself a model of good citizenship in terms of supporting the central chancellery. It led in behaving as a constructive and productive part of the federated UWS rather than inclining towards separatism. Financial, student and other quantitative indicators over the next several years demonstrated the success with which Nepean moved beyond the crisis phase into healthy new development with a vibrant, satisfying environment.

Meanwhile, Macarthur and Hawkesbury continued to grow and to build on their unique histories and strengths. There was some continuing legacy of internal UWS system competition and duplication of resources, but very significant enhancement of size, profile and output despite the difficult times for all universities that had set in with the change of federal government in mid-1996 and subsequent tampering with funding and student numbers.

New leadership, new style and direction

The big crisis for UWS was thus confronted when it occurred in mid-1995 and resolved before the end of the following year. When a new vice-chancellor and president of UWS took office in May 1998, she set out to create synergies and rationalize some services, especially in big management information system driven areas, through a strategic planning processes called Agenda 2000. This created a lot of committee work, employed external consultants and did a lot of planning. Virtually nothing was actually done as a result, however, and time was lost revisiting decisions and having different parties debate often duplicate and sometimes cancel one another's work.

The following year a decision was taken instead to amalgamate the three members into a unitary 'new UWS', emulating the naming device used to launch the 'new Nepean' in 1997. The result was a very detailed paper called *The Shape of the Future*, which too was followed and carried forward via a very large number of working parties and planning mechanisms, again with substantial outside consultant involvement. This paper first appeared in its final form at the governing board of trustees in September 1999. The contrast with the Nepean restructuring process, which grew out of a widely based 'deep slice' day long conference in December 1996 and was then shaped through time-framed but patently diverse and participatory modes of development, was striking.

The analogous 1999 UWS restructure started earlier in the year but rather than bedding down for the comparable new (2001) academic year was still in full swing with no end in sight a year later. The 2002 academic year was heralded by another series of internal contortions, with embarrassing external publicity.[8] The solution to a crisis made by management had developed into something like permanent crisis. It comes to appear less as crisis management and resolution than as a continuing management style.

Central to the UWS change process was a cascading spill-and-fill, apparently modelled on a similar process in a similar institution on the far side of the country. The unsettling process flowed down through the institution and was still going on two years later. The three member presidents who welcomed the new vice-chancellor in May 1998 all left, along with a fourth who succeeded the first to go and resigned in 2001. Many experienced administrators, academic and professional, left with redundancy pay-outs. Some involved protracted litigation. Several other senior new appointments made through this process also soon left. The three human resource managers and heads of public relations units were displaced but the two new central UWS appointments made to these areas both soon resigned.

Many well regarded academic, professional and administrative staff, especially in high-demand areas, left of their own will, some to more senior positions nearby. UWS had initially attracted senior academic staff from older institutions who found its potential fresh and challenging. Now there was a rapid net export of the most mobile, adept and skilled senior as well as junior talent. The size of the professoriate diminished dramatically (assisting lower budget expenditure targets to be met in the immediate term). Hesitancy and preoccupation with restructuring meant long delays with the annual promotion cycle, and further loss of experienced capable people taking institutional memory and know-how with them.

The cost of crisis as a management style and mode of control

A multifaceted crisis quickly spiralled from the addressing of a crisis that did not really exist. The real crisis was resolved earlier. What now happened, putting a public relations spin on a somewhat disastrous situation, was billed as the biggest restructure in the history of Australian higher education. It resulted in single-minded pre-occupation with *The Shape of the Future* to the exclusion of almost everything else. External partnerships and community liaisons, which constituted the UWS's unique strength and greatest asset, were neglected.[9]

A fund of goodwill for these changes and for the personable new vice-chancellor quickly turned sour. The intranet website discussion board for the restructure was initially lively but soon ceased to function when no response was visible. In its dying days a critical question was posted. Would there be any reply from a listening management? Other internal communication devices were created and also soon abandoned. The contributions of elected staff members to trustees turned from warm support to sharp criticism, with alarming feedback about declining morale, confusion and administrative errors. Student unions undertook various forms of direct action. They won regular media publicity unflattering to the university. The staff unions took industrial action on several occasions over failure to conduct effective bargaining for the Third Round Enterprise Agreement. An unblemished UWS record of industrial harmony was decisively altered. Union membership rose sharply and, despite decimation of union leadership, trust and cooperation faded.

The university became locally almost invisible apart from bad press stories. Community leaders no longer knew whom to approach. The university suffered a hostile local press, which is important in the Western suburbs. Word-of-mouth narrative was if anything more harmful. A university with 31,000 mostly local students and a staff of several thousand has extensive networks. Few in the region did not know someone who was in some way part of the university.

One indicator of organizational health and morale is the circulating stories and myths. Myth is vital to institutional health and identity. Gossip can be humorously supportive and generous to the foibles of management as long as there is confidence in the leadership. Or it can be cruel and pointed. At UWS stories of cars, refurbishments and other indulgences were an indicator of damaged morale rather than necessarily in the main of the vice-chancellor's behaviour. A joke circulating over two years after *The Shape of the Future* was launched asked what was the difference between UWS and the *Titanic*. Answer: the *Titanic* was going forward when it went down.

A wounding campaign by students and staff adopted a slogan from a popular TV programme. *Not Happy Jan* lapel badges were worn widely, though some kept them in office drawers from fear of reprisal. The vice-chancellor's distinctively first person singular communications attracted rising cynicism as 'spin-doctoring'. Tales of interference, inefficiency and indecision circulated in increasing volume. Particular suspicion attached to the processes of removing and replacing staff. Charges of cronyism affronted the equity tradition in which UWS took pride.

More damaging was the sense that restructuring was never-endingly disruptive: not in the purposeful sense claimed for Maoist perpetual revolution, but because deadlines were forever missed. Real-world requirements got overlooked and caused difficulties for staff and students.[10]

Why did it happen, and with what results?

Such behaviour may be caused by low self-confidence, low tolerance of ambiguity, high risk aversion and an urge for tight control of detail, often called micro-managing, and also by the incapability to delegate and trust others. An informal inner cabal or 'court cabinet' is seen as making the real decisions. Those down the long line of authority from very senior to junior share the experience of being disempowered. All but the most trivial decisions migrate upwards. Preoccupation with dignity of office can make thing worse, and the need to control makes for an instinct to manage upwards. Worry about taking decisions leads to excessive hiring of consultants on all kinds of matters.

Aspirations to create new partnerships and directions fell away one after another. The 2000 Olympics were held in the UWS region. Despite planning nothing was done that was not already in place. Plans for a UWS Ethnic Council went into limbo. The important and highly sensitive area of Aboriginal development became highly problematic rather than a lighthouse for new approaches. A Greater Western Sydney Learning Network failed to use special funds allocated for the purposes granted. The senior professor appointed to lead the project resigned from the project and the university, fearful for his own reputation. These more visionary ideas for a distinctive university fell away as the restructuring generated in-house work avoiding wider questions.

A significant decision significantly reduced over-enrolment. The federal administration pays a much smaller annual grant (about 25 per cent) for students enrolled above an agreed number to allow the filling of places at marginal cost. A few new places have also been fully funded on the basis of demand and performance. This is a generous regime compared with the UK maximum aggregate student number penalty system. UWS had grown fast in line with its mission and the low age participation rate of GWS, using this elbow room and playing to win new fully funded places over time. Quite suddenly it became unfashionable to over-enrol. Not that it was vetoed. But the government informally signalled that it no longer favoured this system. Instead it hinted that over-enrolment in response to high demand and funded at the marginal rate was a sign of declining quality.

UWS quickly fell into line, unsubstantiated though the allegation of reduced quality had been. It set itself lower annual targets. Short-term conformity contradicted an explicit, formally approved mission to expand, and to raise the low age participation rate of its disadvantaged and under-participating region, in trying to appease an unsympathetic government. In the longer term this will prove costly. In this case high-control micro-management favoured a tendency to reduce size and complexity to something that could be managed. It did not end the culture of crisis perpetuation.

A research review in 2001, acclaimed as the biggest and most thorough in Australian university history, had a similar outcome. External experts dominated by a classic sandstone research perspective predictably recommended concentration in a few areas of established performance at a cost to emergent growth areas. Despite asserted fitness for purpose there was no obvious correlation between regional needs and the areas to be supported. The result promises to be a further tendency to approximate the norm, inevitably at the bottom end, rather than strike out in original and more fitting directions.[11] One emeritus professor described the decision as courageous, in an unintended echo of Whitehall's Sir Humphrey.[12]

The vice-chancellor reported on the restructuring of UWS to an overseas administrators' conference in late 2001. The abstract describes UWS as 'the only institution which [previously] effectively resisted a full merger'. It thus followed a conventional unquestioning stance to federation at just the time when such models are being looked at with fresh interest elsewhere as a possible way of handling large scale and diversity.

The federation was, the abstract asserts, 'beset by internal competition and the growing threat of disintegration'; hence the rationale for 'far-reaching reorganization'. In fact, the crisis peaked and was resolved earlier. The 'periods of industrial unrest and student protests' were brought on by and followed the restructure. They were not a cause of it.[13]

This abstract betrays a misperception that change was being managed with sensitivity to values and past achievements, using celebration and symbols. The perception from a representative staff perspective on trustees differed sharply. Paraphrasing, 'clear principles' are interpreted to mean 'whom do my minder and I like this week?' As to communication, 'how long since an announcement of a new staff member was made?' 'When was the last entry on the forum?' Or, more importantly, 'what division of communications and marketing?' Flexibility translates as 'whoops, another stuff-up – I'll have to back-track again'. Symbolic celebrations translate as 'demonstrations, strikes and Not happy Jan'. The gulf between perception abroad and among workers back home illustrates how in all innocence crisis is made and sustained, rather than managed and brought to an end.

'The literature of crisis'

This chapter started by asking what crises are, and how and why they are made. Real crises are times and events for action rather than rumination. It may take courage to ask questions at such a time. The inhibition on asking questions is one reason for having a crisis, if management is about control.

A literature on crises naturally concerns itself mainly with real crises, rather than chronic difficulty or stage-managed events. Journals devoted to the subject include *Contemporary Crisis* and the *Journal of Contingencies and Crisis Management*. Others include studies of crisis management, such as *Public Administration* and *Administration and Society*. Indirectly books like *The Neurotic Organization* (Kets de Vries and Miller 1984) consider reasons for crisis making.

An editorial analysis notes the emergence of scholarly study of crisis management from the exotic and the dramatic to include 'the complexities and intricacies of adhocracy, groupthink, personal stress'. Now 'crises are no longer seen as events with a clear-cut beginning and a distinct cut-off point. They are viewed as a process . . . because both theory and practice betray an increasing awareness that crisis should be viewed and managed in the context of broader streams of time' (Rosenthal and Kouzmin 1996: 119). That approach is adopted in this chapter.

The same paper notes that 'crisis management increasingly

extends its endeavours to so-called creeping crises', calling for 'the typical qualities of genuine institutions being able to redeem and cash in on the values they represent'. The destruction of institution and institutional memory that goes with repeated restructuring reduces the capacity to manage real crises.

Another paper notes the tendency to centralize in the face of crisis and concentrate power in a small group. It notes that 'crises, whether exogenous, self-imposed or even "wilful" [the kind profiled in this case study], may bring about a widely felt need for strong leadership and a show of decisional resolve', along with neurotic organizational behaviours ('tHart *et al.* 1993).

Another study explores the 'increasing dependency on out-sourcing expensive professional support, the extent of the use/abuse of consultants . . . [and] the sheer dramatic rise in the cost of consult-ancies . . . Over re-engineered agencies not only lose their distinctive competencies, but also lose the very capacity for dialogue . . . The on-going failure of many consultant interventions is a policy question that also needs urgent attention' (Korac-Kakabadse *et al.* 1998: 4; see also Duke 2002). The high but never made public cost and low yield from external consultants (including a high level of costly legal advice) was a feature of the UWS case of self-imposed crisis. Loss of capacity for dialogue was amplified by the perception that only paid-for outside expertise could be trusted and used.

A further study explores 'alternative paths available to an organiza-tion that is in a crisis state to move away from crisis back to more routine modes of operation' (Jarman and Kouzmin 1990: 399–400). It criticizes reductionism and omniscience, both economistic and psychologistic, in decision-making literature for downgrading rele-vant complexity. Renormalizing things requires empowering people to act with purpose and confidence, avoiding the micro-management that paralyses and disempowers. It means keeping an eye on 'the devil in the detail', and living with the ambiguity of *both–and*, not *either–or*, the paradox that black is often also white.

Other places, similar events: is there no choice?

Widespread and burgeoning managerialism

Not all Australian universities make crises in trying to manage com-plexity within uncertainty. There is by all accounts an increasing tendency to adopt what is commonly called managerialism: tighter executive control, a shift from shared authority and collegiality to line command. Increasingly powerful and sophisticated information systems are used to measure and control against internal targets and wider benchmarks. Quite often this is accompanied by a growing cult of leadership. Management becomes more the prerogative of office, less the privilege of participatory leadership. An institution's social capital declines as 'human resources' become human capital in a human capital production factory.

Examples from different institutions illustrate the trend. One vice-chancellor withdrew the use of e-mail from a member of academic staff who used the intranet to criticize decisions of university council, of which he was a member. This triggered the formation of an association to defend academic freedom. Another dismissed a tenured member of staff for asserting to the media that he had been required to soften his marking to raise the pass rate. The academic union (the NTEU) placed a ban on the university with the support of sister bodies overseas. His case was won in the industrial commission, which required that he be reinstated.

Two other vice-chancellors in confrontation with the NTEU over third round enterprise bargaining went direct to staff with a ballot to undermine the union as representative. Both were heavily defeated and returned weakened to the negotiating table. Two vice-chancellors suffered hostile media exposure over the purchase of corporate entertainment boxes at major sports venues. In one case, for the 2000 Olympics, the incident is held to have been a factor in non-extension of contract.

At a fifth university the incoming vice-chancellor removed all the senior management and appointed entirely new senior staff. At another within a few months the last surviving dean to pre-date the incoming vice-chancellor had resigned. At a seventh almost the first public act of the promoted deputy was to remove the other deputy from office, then make life systematically uncomfortable in other ways. A pattern emerges that resembles the American presidency, in which the spoils of office include appointment to executive positions. The convention that protected the executive administration in an earlier tradition and echoes the classic separation of powers gives way to putting in place one's own team.

More obvious is the urge to restructure. Each new chief executive reshapes the future to fit their imagining of what a good university looks like, and how they would like it to be run. The costs are rarely considered and still more rarely if ever measured. They include not just visible redundancy payouts, recruitment and induction costs, and the changes to systems, letterheads etc. that flow from changed designations, but also the less measurable and perhaps higher costs in loss of institutional memory and weakened morale.

In one of the cases above, a uniquely qualified private practitioner had negotiated an electronically based mixed mode masters in a leading edge field. The perturbations and loss of personnel, understanding and memory caused by restructuring in that university were so disruptive that the project was lost. Soon after this he moved across country to Sydney. A personal link with a UWS professor as doctoral supervisor led into initially fruitful negotiations there. An excellent agreement involving a medically strong university and a major hospital was fashioned. Then the UWS preoccupation with *The Shape of the Future* stopped this, along with other outside partnerships. Once again the course was aborted at the point of take-off. The contact professor left for a more satisfying appointment elsewhere.[14]

Rewriting history

At another university the vice-chancellor some time before completion of the first contract period had a striking full-length portrait painted and hung alongside those of his predecessors: not only did it feature a snake at the vice-chancellor's feet but it was twice the size of the other portraits, painted more traditionally after completion of service. The media made some play of the dramatic effect, revisiting it cruelly when the individual resigned suddenly not much later. The successor, past master of crisis management, announced that the university faced bankruptcy within a short time and that the central office was hugely over-staffed. He immediately put steps in train to move most of these staff out 'where there was work to be done'.

A more public charge of rewriting history featured in the press when Steven Schwartz, the outgoing vice-chancellor of Murdoch University, described the problems he inherited and how he solved the crisis. So provocative was his account that the following week long letters were published in the same newspaper by the previous vice-chancellor and the previous registrar, comprehensively refuting the account. The former vice-chancellor, in a letter spanning six columns, comments apropos of the 'self-congratulatory review' that 'a respect for historical accuracy seems to have deserted him at times', the claims being 'wide of the mark'. Perhaps he failed to give due recognition to the pace and extent of changes prior to his arrival; the 'sweeping accusations about accountability' were 'breathtaking'. 'Perhaps,' he concludes, 'Vice-Chancellors are not the most appropriate historians and assessors of their own performance.' The former registrar is similarly scathing, finding what he calls uninformed insinuation and inference 'both unfair and incorrect' (*The Australian* 2001a, b).

This was blunt even by Australian standards. The incident echoed the less public one in which the UWS vice-chancellor made it known how serious a problem she claimed to have inherited as a result of predecessor inaction. The chancellor felt obliged to retract for the record at the board of trustees. The former head of public relations had a letter published in the national media refuting the imputed slur on the previous vice-chancellor's management. Is rewriting history to make a crisis where none existed more characteristic of crisis-making than managing crisis?[15]

Some lessons for management and leadership

Nice day for a restructure – or is it?

Almost any structure will work with goodwill and a sense of purpose. Any structure is rendered ineffectual if there is not the will to make it work. It is said that form follows purpose. Why then is restructuring so popular a pastime?

Note this advice: 'many organizations and agencies find the pressure to accept management recipes (restructuring, de-layering, re-engineering, outsourcing) irresistible. The idea that these recipes might not be appropriate is often inconceivable to those managing these organizations and agencies. Yet these same managers should realize that inappropriate management models may foster adversity rather than prosperity, and may indeed solicit their own version of a creeping crisis' (Rosenthal and Kouzmin 1996: 121).

It has become normal for a new vice-chancellor to 'restructure' the university. Fashion changes quickly. Contrasting trends may occur simultaneously. Some universities may be 'delayering' to create a flatter and more flexible structure, others adding a layer by producing colleges or super-faculties to aggregate faculties. Schools may be inserted between faculties and departments, or introduced in place of either, or more unusually of both.

The rationale for the change is not always clear. Tighter hierarchical command aligns with a more managerial approach, but can also be intended to enable devolution and local autonomy. The danger is that devolution to budget-holding entities, whether called colleges, faculties or schools, creates new silos, more opportunities for authoritarian management and loss of central steerage. It thus contradicts the guidance drawn by Burton Clark from his case studies and follow-up work on 'the entrepreneurial university'.

As interesting as the rationale for restructure is what its timing tells us in the context of managing crisis. A change of leadership may be an opportunity (and so 'a critical moment'). It should not be a crisis. Restructure marking the arrival of a new head may, however, engender a crisis or a downward spiral of disruption, lowering energy, morale and performance. If the purpose is seen as stamping authority, making a mark, rather than addressing an agreed need to change, the reception may be cool and a crisis may be induced.

The change of structure at UWS Nepean grew out of a hideously public crisis. Subsequently, faculty deans with executive power came to behave with rebellious independence – the term feral was in use. A change of structure removing both deans and faculties responded to a need for open internal and external networking. The resulting flat participatory structure generated measurably enhanced collaboration. Indisputable bottom-line gains within two years were underpinned by qualitative changes in culture and morale. Cultural change masquerading as structural gave a handle to the more important change. A benevolent spiral of energy generation continued to show in bottom-line results until the distinct identity of the institution was usurped and disappeared.

It was just over a year before the new UWS leader introduced a proposal to amalgamate the three cultures and identities into a single structure. The ground was prepared while the intent to merge was being denied. The merger followed on classic industrial lines. The almost universal perception of the processes and choices encumbered the confidence-building essential to create a new merged institutional identity.

The restructuring appears, with the short hindsight of two and a half years, to have created and sustained a crisis, with tight yet ineffectual control and neurotic disruption as a continuing state. The cost shows especially in loss of external credibility and distinctive competence through regional support and productive working partnerships. The claim that this was the biggest restructuring in Australian history speaks about its function and the motivation behind it.

Many new institutional heads in Australia today incline to 'restructuring' as an early act. An interesting contrast is provided by Edinburgh, where such a change (used by the OECD as a case study in training institutional heads) came late in Sir Stuart Sutherland's incumbency. Newcastle has more conventionally (in current terms) restructured as an early act of a new head. In Australia the Newcastle pattern is commoner, although coincidentally the Australian namesake university has carried through a change of structure well into the incumbency of the present vice-chancellor.

A real crisis such as Huddersfield and Thames Valley experienced, and University College Cardiff much earlier, may call for major structural change if dysfunctional structure is at the heart of the problem. Usually, though, it is a failure of leadership and culture, leading to a breakdown of institutional confidence and self-confidence, rather than of structure.

Do different kinds of university have different kinds of crisis, and if so, why?

The huge diversity of universities, even within relatively conventional meanings, setting aside for example the corporate and the virtual universities, means that few generalizations will fit each unique case. Different kinds of universities may address crises in different ways.

Cambridge had an embarrassing and financially costly crisis in 2001 over the introduction of new management software. The consultant who had handled the Cardiff crisis reviewed the situation for the VC and identified the particular and possibly peculiar fault-line that Cambridge walked (Shattock 2001): a strong vice-chancellor calling in a tough consultant to address the problem. Whether a crisis or an embarrassing hiccup, this offered no survival threat to Britain's top research university. The same event and financial cost might have marked the end for a weak and impoverished institution whose card was already marked by a funding council.

A related question is: whose responsibility is it to manage crises, between management, governance and leadership? The Great Leader, the modern presidential Australian chief executive, for example, assumes this role. Yet in many Australian universities, where history, practice and constitutionality give a different context, the chancellor, and by implication the governing body that the chancellor chairs, may exercise power and authority unknown in Britain except in some ex-polytechnic universities.

The UWS chancellor was highly supportive of the vice-chancellor, and kept the trustees reassured, isolating critical elected staff and student members. Elsewhere it is a different story. Despite the dramatic and very public removal of the Sydney chancellor in 2001, she had already seen off the previous vice-chancellor. The University of New England chancellor removed the UNE vice-chancellor a little earlier, as did the Southern Cross chancellor, though he also went down in the attempt. The new chancellor of Adelaide soon received the resignation of the incumbent vice-chancellor whose portrait had been so early painted and hung. Given the privacy and sensitivity of such matters this may be the tip of the iceberg.

It is obvious that different contexts make for differences in the politics and power equation. Discussion of stronger governance in the UK might helpfully be informed by this comparative perspective. Whose crisis is it, and whose solution? What is the price of a competitive division of powers?[16]

The bigger picture: systems in crisis

There are crises and crises

Taking a particular case study, this chapter suggests that crisis can be manufactured and sustained as a dysfunctional mode of exercising control. The cost is a destabilized institution less capable of autonomous and creative action. Creating and sustaining crisis as a mode of management, rather than managing crisis, may be less uncommon than we should hope, if less obvious than in the example here.

Crises can be used to protect management and divert attention from its frailties. This displaces the true business of management: from enabling a productive organization to be clear about and achieve its purposes, to protecting the power base of management as an end in itself. It tends to be short term, political rather than strategic. Ultimately it courts self-defeat. The rapid turnover of vice-chancellors in many of today's universities may be connected. Being fleet-footed keeps you ahead of the recognition of a litany of mistakes and of their consequences

If crisis is our normal condition, as can be argued for most universities and higher education systems, 'having a crisis' does not excuse bad management. There are unique crises in the more accepted disaster sense. But the chronic crisis of a system changing from elite through to universal and higher into tertiary means that the word is misused. Like the management of change, the management of crisis is now normal management. It means facilitating institutional self-management to handle continuous, complex, interactive and largely unpredictable change – what Barnett (2000) calls supercomplexity.

System development to avert crisis

Taking a wider view, the truly chronic crisis *is* systemic. As idiosyncratically different universities are pulled into centrally steered tertiary *systems*, special heritage and other assets come under threat. Homogenization may destroy what gives each university distinctive life and character over time. Purposeful re-engineering, especially the removal of inherited wisdom and senior management, accelerates the process. The ways, myths and resilience of most universities are, however, buried deep enough in the infrastructure to be able to outlast most short-stay chief executives.

Crises can be avoided by appropriate strategies, both system and institutional. This means altering the current tendency to standardize and so homogenize. It means much more effective support for intra-system diversity, so that different forms of contribution are valued, rewarded and celebrated publicly and within the institution. It favours a profiling methodology of funding universities rather than one based on common performance competitively judged across all the same standard-measured performance indicators. Each institution must persuade those with funds of the propriety of their particular mission. Common benchmarks, now international as well as national, drive in the wrong direction. Winners take all, the weaker go to the wall, many clienteles and societal needs are neglected.

This requires each leader and each self-managing institution – as a hive of creative knowledge workers contributing in different ways to the knowledge society – to excel at their own purposes in the best fitted ways. Instead of having a manufactured crisis – whether Falklands or restructuring – it demands the toughness of real *leadership*, without 'the prerogatives of management' and trappings of office, participatively to create, share and have owned and actualized a vision for the unique university in its unique setting. It means cutting a new road, not following others down their roads in another place. System planners in funding councils, tertiary commissions and departments of education will prevent excessive straying.

Seen thus, UWS brings to a focus the need for more different models for managing big systems. Multiple modes of affiliation, partnership, federation and other linkages are needed, as well as diversities of mission. Dual sector institutions are one good Australian alternative. There has been increasing interest in such matters in the UK of late, as well as caution. We lack and urgently need a *system matrix* of institutional purposes and forms (with form following purpose) that enables non-dominant productive diversity, despite the unavoidable, not in itself unhealthy, competitive tendency.

The lost opportunity

The tragedy of UWS is that it represented a really interesting institutional form. It was irritating but in many senses it worked well, as UWS Nepean indicators show. It could have developed as a model able to accommodate growth and diversity, which its big region needs. Six rising to eight sub-regional responsive boutique campus communities offered the benefits of bigness (sixth largest in the country but now below nineth) with intimacy. The fact that the other two post-1989 federated systems had defaulted, one to integration, the other to dissolution, and the fright of 1995, although put firmly to rest, pointed to a conventional way out, masquerading as courage. The road taken was the road well walked in the past by others in other places. The model was abandoned too easily. Widely shared and evident goodwill to make the new UWS work dissipated over two years.

One essay in diversity in a relatively homogenous system has been lost. It is to be hoped that, as UK universities come under pressure to grow larger, and individually and collectively to meet yet more diverse missions, common sense, courage and integrity may combine to find better networked, federated and affiliating means of managing scale, without creating impersonal bureaucracies that destroy character and community but may seem to make the life of the top manager easier. This could ameliorate the chronic crisis, releasing energy to deal with real crises when they do occur, as from time to time they surely will.

Notes

1 More detail of the changes, especially at UWS Nepean, may be found in Duke (2000, 2001a, b). See also Latham (2001) for a sketch of how the 'old UWS' could and should have worked well.
2 Although local distances required vice-chancellor Schreuder to hire a helicopter to show the visiting higher education (west) review team all campuses in one visit, it is all very local by Australian standards.
3 Hawkesbury, the smallest, an old agricultural college, acquired a second campus at Blacktown as part of UWS, whereas Macarthur, the former Milperra CAE, brought with it the Bankstown and Campbelltown campuses. Nepean, the largest and geographically centred, brought its Penrith and Parramatta campuses, along with a third Westmead campus and a small Sydney central business district facility.
4 Two-thirds of UWS Nepean students were first in family in higher education, and 40 per cent came from homes where English was not the spoken language. Graduation days led by a passionately dedicated chancellor were multicultural and multigenerational celebrations of great character and exuberance.
5 Since then it has fallen below ninth place. The claim that this shrinkage enhanced quality was negated by the public January 2002 (*Sydney Morning Herald*) entry cut-off scores for all NSW universities, which showed UWS clearly lowest on this (however flawed and limited) public indicator. Transparent public league tables such as those *The Times* publishes are not available in this way in Australia, other than in an annual private *Good Universities Guide*.

6 Professor Brian Smith was followed in 1994 by Professor Deryck Schreuder, who left in 1998 to become vice-chancellor of the 'sandstone' University of Western Australia. Despite his own sandstone University of Sydney lineage Schreuder was able to resonate well with the 'Westies' of GWS, where he became widely known, liked and even revered. His successor, who took office in May 1998, has not sustained this regional visibility and is little known.

7 Although different in detail, this, together with the system for stimulating and managing entrepreneurial 'earned income', borrowed heavily on experience and models from Warwick. For other information about the processes and outcomes involved in overcoming the crisis and building the 'new Nepean' see Duke (2001a, b).

8 On this occasion the 'new UWS' reactivated a requirement on students not achieving a certain grade point average in 2001 to 'show cause' why they should not be excluded, an arrangement abandoned following academic policy review at Nepean some years earlier, and probably not legal to introduce for students part-way through their courses. A genuine new crisis was caused. Some 6300 students were threatened with exclusion, with too little time to cope with the unanticipated consequences. Individual counselling was rationed to a half hour to try to cope. A satirical letter was sent to the vice-chancellor and beyond. This mimicked the letter the 6300 students received, advising her of a low 2001 grade point average with supporting transcript, and urging counselling. Worse, a rumour circulated that the whole episode was a stratagem to reduce student numbers, making the university smaller and easier to manage.

9 Even in 2002 the urge to control continued to inhibit the rebuilding of effective partnerships. A reiterated 'correct protocol' insisted that invitations on to any campus of even local government ministers and members (that is to say, humble councillors and their officers), as well as royalty and the vice-regal, must be 'extended in writing by the vice-chancellor' for any event, function or even to look at facilities.

10 One of the worst in 2001 concerned confused examination schedules arising from ill thought through changes to the academic year. The resulting chaotic mess was exacerbated by loss of tacit knowledge. The resulting radio and press attention was unhelpful in terms of both academic quality and efficiency. A student hotline was set up but under someone already made redundant in conflictual circumstances. A suggestion to alter marking of the work of students affected courted another crisis with the new Quality Agency.

11 Unlike publicity in the general media through 2000–1 this research review earned a favourable front page spread in the specialized weekly *Campus Review* (12 January 2002). The reform is featured as bold and exciting, leading to a 'substantial research university' over the next decade. It may also mean doing poorly what others do better, while neglecting essential work that UWS alone can do.

12 It is a further measure of cynicism after two years of crisis that *Campus Review* is suspect to some at UWS, its editor being the partner of the UWS senior deputy vice-chancellor. There is no evidence that its editorial policy is thus influenced.

13 See below on the rewriting of history. The only serious reprimand from the chancellor to trustees was for denigrating the predecessor vice-chancellor in painting a favourable picture of management in the 'new UWS'. Rewriting history to explain progress beyond others' crisis and failure is not unusual.

14 Succession crises constitute a significant theme in the crisis literature, but according to Kouzmin most of the research is out of corporate experience rather than from the institutional perspective of, for example, Phil Selznick (Alexander Kouzmin, personal correspondence).

15 The UWS vice-chancellor's 2002 budget referred to 'internal inefficiencies' and projected financial deterioration as a rationale for the restructuring, which in large part created the problematic conditions.

16 The division of powers is actually three-way in Australia to an extent unfamiliar in the UK. The (academic) senate is commonly chaired by an elected senior member of academic staff and has a separate office and infrastructure. Thus a check-and-balance situation exists both above and below the vice-chancellor. This may help to explain the stronger urge towards presidential style and power in Australia, but does make the cure better than the malady.

10

A FUNDING COUNCIL PERSPECTIVE
Brian Fender

Introduction

The aim of this chapter is to describe the managing of crises in universities and higher education colleges through the eyes of a former chief executive of the Higher Education Funding Council for England (HEFCE). It is a personal perspective and not an official Funding Council view. The chapter is in four main sections. The first part describes the role of HEFCE. The second section analyses how and why the risks facing higher education institutions have increased. The third part describes how the policies and practices of HEFCE have developed to help universities to deal with a changing and more challenging higher education world. The fourth part describes more particularly how the HEFCE works to reduce the risk of crisis and how it helps universities or colleges to deal with them when they arise.

Funding Council responsibilities

The Funding Council has undergone several transformations since the University Grants Committee (UGC) was created in 1920, but its statutory role of distributing public money to universities and colleges remains (HEFCE 2002c). What does this mean in practice? In simple terms it means promoting an overall programme for the sector that delivers good value for money for the taxpayer. This in turn has three consequences. One is to find funding mechanisms that encourage individual universities to develop their strengths. The second is to set in place an accountability regime that reduces the risk of failure and financial loss. Third, but by no means least, there is a requirement to advise government of the needs and potential of higher education and to point up to students and the public more widely the opportunities provided by higher education.

The traditional early role of the UGC was as a buffer between universities and the government, and the pace of that relationship was exemplified by quinquennial submissions of a university's achievements and ambitions. The funding provided was opaque but reliable; national negotiations involving the government determined salary levels, and grant supplements followed to cater for the cost of those settlements and for inflation. Furthermore, the predictable flow of annual grants was occasionally spiced by funding to cover a special development. The level of funding per student looks generous by today's standards and there was a steady expansion of fully funded student numbers in the post-Robbins era. This was as near to a crisis-free era for universities as one is ever likely to achieve. The modern higher education sector is very different and we need to examine why HEFCE, which provides an ever smaller proportion of universities' total income, is more prominent in the day-to-day life of universities than ever before.

Increased pressures and risks for the contemporary university

The job of vice-chancellor is now one of the most demanding of chief executive positions. It is highly visible, as the performance of the university is intensively scrutinized and the markets in which universities operate become ever more competitive. Many vice-chancellors would concede that a potential crisis is possible if not probable and the Funding Council is likely to have concerns not just about a university's financial position but also about the academic programme, its appeal to students, the quality of its management and the strength of its income-raising activities.

Let us look at the changes in higher education that have increased the levels of risk that a university faces.

Increased involvement of government

The expansion of higher education brought about by successive governments inevitably brings increased responsibility for HEIs. Higher education is a key part of the UK's economy and with more than 1.6 million students there are large swathes of the population who have a direct engagement. Awarding student loans instead of grants, charging up front fees to the better off, as in England, or not, as in Scotland, as well as the actual level of fees demanded are strong political issues. But if the government leans towards minimizing the burden for students or parents there will be less money for institutions.

The government also has policy targets and the implementation of these does of course have strategic and financial impact on universities. The present government's primary concern is widening participation. There is a clear target that, by 2010, 50 per cent of the population aged 18–30 will be participating or will have participated in higher education (DfES 2001). This target favours those universities with well developed plans for recruiting students from disadvantaged backgrounds but conversely increases the risk that funding will not be available for universities whose strategic priorities lie elsewhere.

There are also risks to a university's reputation. Widening participation has spawned a raft of performance indicators (HEFCE 2001i), which include intakes from low participation neighbourhoods, state schools and non-completion rates. Although the Funding Councils provide benchmarks to relate an individual institution's performance to an expected performance based on its student population, there is little doubt that the information on non-completion in particular intensifies the already sensitive market for the recruitment of students.

Governments too are increasingly sensitive to their reputation for good management and particularly to press criticisms that are directed at the government of the day even when the responsibility has been clearly delegated. As a result, even though universities receive less than 60 per cent of their funding directly from the public purse they are now more likely to receive attention from the National Audit Office and in some cases the Public Accounts Committee. Universities have very rarely been accused of any financial impropriety and there have been no cases of major misdemeanours, but the effects of an inquiry like those involving Portsmouth University and Southampton Institute (Public Accounts Committee 1999) can create disproportionate disruption to the running of the university.

The student market

The change in the student market represents the largest change facing university managements. During the rapid expansion of the university population in the late 1980s and early 1990s universities could grow easily and concerns about student recruitment were minimal except in a few subjects. Now the availability of university places slightly exceeds the number of qualified places. That in itself does not seem threatening but, coupled with quite big year-on-year changes in the popularity of different areas of study, a small number of universities (and more further education colleges for their HE programmes) do underrecruit each year in total numbers and many more will have a less than optimum distribution of students across disciplines.

In fact, despite popular perceptions, there is from the perspective of HEIs very nearly a free market in student demand. It is true that some institutions could expand very considerably, but only by lowering undergraduate entry qualifications below a level they consider acceptable. Nevertheless, the consequence of a free market is that there is a risk that some universities will have an academic portfolio that is not in tune with student demand.

The well publicized cut in the unit of resource for UK students has pushed universities to look for an expansion of activities beyond the education of UK and EU undergraduates. That coincides with a very strong demand for postgraduate courses and a growth in the worldwide total of students seeking an education abroad. British universities have responded very well to these trends but the risks are greater than for undergraduate recruitment.

Privately financed overseas students were affected by the Asian financial downturn in the late 1990s and could be affected by international terrorism. Postgraduate education too is often privately financed and the demand is probably more susceptible to fluctuations than that for undergraduate education, which has more obvious financial rewards for the student.

Arguably the biggest perturbation in the student market in future will come from e-learning. Many universities already supplement learning on campus with a range of computer-based material. The availability of educational materials over the Internet threatens traditional pedagogies. It more obviously extends the distance learning market, for so long dominated in the UK by the Open University, particularly to overseas markets and to corporate programmes like the British Aerospace 'University' and the 'University' of the NHS. But successful courses developed in the UK for these markets are bound also to be available on UK campuses. So the home student market becomes defined in terms of not just the number of enrolled students but also the proportion of the academic programme produced and delivered in-house.

Research

The greatest impact universities over the past 20 years has came from the Research Assessment Exercise (RAE) (see www.hero.ac.uk/rae). Designed by the UGC under Sir Peter Swynnerton-Dyer and introduced to account for the UGC's substantial allocation of research funding, it also provides universities, and others, with a clear quality benchmark. Its effect is greatest on universities that aim to be research intensive and the strongest universities at research have gained considerably from an allocation that is the most selective in the world.

There is no doubt that the RAE has very substantially improved university research and greatly increased its professionalism. But it has two important downsides. One is that for university groups that do not have a large proportion of research of international calibre (5 and 5*) there is a big reduction in funding, and for universities that are overall light on internationally ranked research there is a risk of being caught in the 'squeezed middle', i.e. falling between those with strong and successful missions based on research (and teaching) and those that choose to concentrate on teaching strengths. The results of the RAE lead to an allocation of around £5 billion of funding for research in England. In fact this is still only about one-third of the total funding universities receive for research but – unfortunately – the esteem attached to research performance spills over in a way that affects the reputation of a department or university more generally. This has a consequence for the quality and quantity of student recruitment.

Quality assessment and league tables

The fourth major pressure on universities and a resultant intensification of competition has arisen from a wish, by the Conservative government in the early 1980s, to see some assessment of teaching quality. Universities responded by setting up the Higher Education Quality Council (HEQC) to audit the processes by which universities and colleges delivered their teaching and learning, but this proved insufficient for a government anxious to see some measure of the quality of teaching. The Funding Councils were therefore charged with devising a system that would give information to students about the quality of teaching provided and would be sufficiently robust to allow the councils to reward good teaching and remove funding from unsatisfactory provision. The different national territories followed slightly different routes but the result was that the quality of teaching within individual universities, like research, became much more transparent. In 1996, after lobbying by the Committee of Vice-chancellors and Principals, the separate processes of audit and assessment were combined in a new higher education Quality Assurance Agency (QAA) (see www.qaa.ac.uk). There is little doubt that these formal quality assurance procedures have improved teaching, but the extra information available to schools, parents and prospective students has made students more selective, putting those higher education institutions with weaker provision more at risk.

The Teacher Training Agency (TTA) (see www.tta.ac.uk) assesses the quality of training for teachers through the agency of OFSTED and has in recent years been assertive in distributing training places based on the results. These consequential reduction in funding, for colleges of higher education in particular, has had a destabilizing effect that has in a few cases contributed to a crisis for the institution as a whole.

One of the consequences of the much greater availability of information is the plethora of league tables produced by the national press (e.g. see *The Times* 10 May 2002). Such tables are far from rigorous, often mixing input information such as spending on libraries and computing, research income and the availability of residential accommodation with outputs such as the results of the teaching and research assessments and completion rates. The weighting adopted for the different parameters used in compiling the tables is of course a matter of judgement and sometimes controversial. Nevertheless, it would be surprising if they did not add to the competitiveness of the student market.

HEFCE policies and practices aimed at the development of higher education in England

The main thrust of the HEFCE strategy in recent years has been to encourage universities and colleges to develop their individual strengths. It has also been involved in developing greater capacity and improved quality in teaching and learning, in research, and particularly over the past two or three years, in knowledge with business and the community. Strengthening these three, often complementary, missions is of course at the heart of the primary aim of the Funding Council, which is to deliver the best possible higher education with the public money available.

But institutions will only be able to achieve this goal if they are realistic about their own strategic strengths and both innovative and easily responsive to change. Much effort is therefore expended by HEFCE in seeking out, disseminating and encouraging good practice, not just in academic areas but also in management and governance. Of course, the benefits of improved performance are reductions in risk to the institution and the smaller chance of a crisis. We will see below how HEFCE practices relate to the four areas of increased risk identified in the first section.

HEFCE actions to improve performance and reduce risk come into several categories as follows:

1 Funding rewards for good performance (e.g. the RAE).
2 Rewarding the development of good practice through a competitive bidding process (e.g. the Fund for the Development of Teaching and Learning).
3 Allocating funding by formula but only releasing the money after certain conditions are met (e.g. the preparation of an acceptable strategic plan for the release of human resource funding).
4 Penalties for failure to meet conditions of a contract (e.g. the under-recruitment of students).
5 The publication of advice.

Each of these different types of action has advantages but also some downsides. Under the RAE a clear scheme of reward for research performance has helped to improve the quality and productivity of university research, but if there is not enough money to reward performance on the same basis as in the past, or if a university has overinvested and underperformed, significant financial embarrassment may occur. Rewarding teaching in a similar way would be far worse. The only way more could be given to strongly performing institutions would be to take it from those that were performing less well, with the creation of substantial instability at the institutional level and certainly no guarantee of improvement for the sector as a whole.

A bidding process will identify good practice either actual or potential, and it is likely to work well to meet specialist needs (e.g. the Chinese studies initiative: HEFCE 1999a), but there are significant disadvantages. There is wasted effort in preparing unsuccessful bids and consequential demotivation for the staff concerned. More fundamentally, the fragmentation of funding could deliver poorer value for money overall than the allocation of the same amount of money to the core grant allocations. But from a risk perspective the main concern is that HEIs may be distracted from their main strategy into chasing money or prestige in more peripheral areas.

A much better funding approach is to identify jointly with institutions a major thematic area for development and to invite the university or college to indicate how it would contribute to the proposal given its size, characteristics and strengths. We have seen this 'partnership funding' extensively applied in recent years to research capital (HEFCE 2002a), teaching strategies (HEFCE 1999b), human resource strategies (HEFCE 2001a) and, in a modified form, the funding of 'third-leg' activities at the interface between academe and business and the community. The advantage of this type of funding is that it reinforces institutional autonomy and, because funding is released only after the approval of the Funding Council, it provides an assurance that the practice within the HEI will be competent and involve little risk.

Funding Councils do have a regulatory role in making sure public money is well spent. They are urged surprisingly often to make compliance with some particular behaviour a 'condition of grant'. In fact, to use funding in such a way would be little short of disastrous. It would be very unlikely that the council would have the confidence in the required practice, outside well tested financial procedures, to make it mandatory. Furthermore, threatening to withhold funds can only act as a deterrent; to implement the threat would only make any situation worse and could precipitate a crisis. Partial withholding of grant would in effect introduce a system of fines, with a reduction or destruction of trust between the Funding Council and the HEI that would be inimical to an effective working partnership. Financial penalties should therefore be enforced only to prevent an institution from benefiting unreasonably from public funds. The most obvious example is failing to recruit students to meet an agreed target. There are also on occasions relatively minor breaches of the financial memorandum (HEFCE 2000a) that governs the formal relationship between HEFCE and the university or college. As far as we are aware, such cases are dealt with rigorously without recourse to any additional financial penalty.

This approach is more important than it seems. Universities are very complex organizations with numerous diverse activities. In the UK, with higher education colleges, their total turnover is over £12 billion and their relationship with the Funding Council, the most important funding body for most HEIs, requires a high degree of trust. The funding methodologies of the councils and their accountability for public money are both very dependent on the flow of high-quality data and information. Even if the audit function were to be greatly increased it is doubtful that the quality of that information could be maintained in a regime based only on compliance. The result would be an increased probability of an institutional crisis.

Over the past decade HEFCE and the other Funding Councils have become more and more prone to give advice. In 2001 this advice ranged, for example, from strategies in teaching and learning (HEFCE

2001e) to the management of student administration (HEFCE 2001c). This is one of the mechanisms to try to capture and disseminate good practice and reduce the chance of HEIs drifting into crisis through lack of knowledge. It is not, however, the role of the Funding Council alone to judge what is good practice; its role is to work with representatives of HEIs to define and illustrate good practice in a form that helps incorporate improved practices into routine operations. There is no doubt that many HEIs find such advice helpful but it is difficult to write advice for such a diverse range of HEIs and there is the danger that the good practice described is seen as *the* good practice and that institutions need look no further, either inside or outside HE, in order to do better.

The HEFCE contribution to managing crises

In this chapter we have identified risks facing the contemporary university and discussed how HEFCE policies and practices in general terms aim to reduce these risks. We now need to assess explicitly the contribution that HEFCE makes to managing crises in the university system. This can be examined through four questions. First, how does HEFCE help to reduce the external risks identified earlier in the chapter? Second, what does the council do to identify and monitor signs of incipient crisis? Third, how does it act to contain the threat of a crisis? Finally, how does it deal with a crisis once it occurs?

Assistance in reducing external risk

Increased involvement of government

The major activities in which universities operate need a relatively long planning horizon. The planning and introduction of a new undergraduate course will take five years before the first students graduate; research teams and reputations can take a decade or more to build and the best partnerships for working with business are likely to take nearly as long. When advising government on the financial needs of the sector it is important for HEFCE to emphasize the medium- and long-term planning requirements.

The prominence of higher education necessitates closer working between HEFCE and the government but, if anything, there is in a period of rapid change an even greater reason for the HEFCE view to be objective and independent. Above all, policies originating from either the government or HEFCE should evolve in an open and consultative manner with enough time for institutions to contribute to the debate and to allow the likely outcome of the discussions to be incorporated into the institution's strategic planning. HEFCE does this best through the publication of its corporate plan (e.g. HEFCE 2002c), through careful attention to individual proposals and ensuing consultation, by signalling key issues through reports of HEFCE board discussions ('Council briefing': see www.hefce.ac.uk) and through the annual conference.

Nevertheless, although the government's policy on widening participation is clear and dovetails with a variety of HEFCE actions, the position on fees has remained confused. Scotland and Wales have abolished up-front fees but they remain in England. Top-up fees are not allowed on full-time undergraduate courses but are on postgraduate and part-time courses. Universities planning strategies on the outcome of this political debate court the risk of future financial problems.

Apart from fees, the publication of three-year projections of public spending has made it easier for the Funding Council to increase the certainty of its annual allocations. Giving as much predictability to future funding as possible is one of the more important steps in encouraging HEIs to plan ahead and to avoid drifting into crisis on the basis of a Micawber-like optimism.

HEFCE's response to concerns about the burdens of too many initiatives has led to a much greater emphasis on the 'partnership' funding described above, and this aspect of better accountability is finding some support in government departments and by the Cabinet Office (2002). Encouraging universities to pursue strategies best suited to their strengths and opportunities is not only sensible but it is likely to lead to better performance and greater stability. Top-down initiatives which curtail that discretion should be avoided unless there is a well articulated and sustainable programme broadly supported by the sector as a whole.

Major crises in universities are, as we have seen, associated with weak management, loss of financial control, a quality failure or a weakness in the student market. But sometimes a relatively minor failing can through adverse publicity be magnified into a significant problem. Partly, this arises from the sensitivity of both the press and the government to quite modest scandals. There are two approaches possible by the Funding Council: one is to intensify the scrutiny of audit process; the other is to improve the management of risk within universities and colleges. The former is very unlikely to be cost-effective, the latter builds on the growing interest of audit committees in risk following the Turnbull Report (1999). The purpose of the HEFCE (2001b, d) publications on risk management is to encourage good practice but also to make the point that all businesses have to take some risk, and if on occasions some ventures lose money that is not in itself a cause for disapprobation if proper risk assessment procedures have been followed. The principal audiences for the latter sentiment are the National Audit Office and the Public Accounts Committee, but some still interpreted the message as a wish by the HEFCE for institutions to be even more risk averse.

The student market

The council's role with respect to the student market is transparent. It is keen to maximize student choice, but not at the expense of quality. It wishes, in line with government policy, to encourage more students to enter higher education. Again in tune with the government's social inclusion policy, it particularly wants to attract students from disadvantaged backgrounds where there is a low probability that a student will progress into higher education. There are a variety of premiums and incentives to encourage this widening participation but the risks are that universities may try to attract students to new courses that are underfinanced or that there are insufficient resources to support students who need additional teaching or extra advice.

The council's response is to require universities to provide a minimum level of resource per student averaged across the university and to fund extra student places through an allocation process (HEFCE 2001f) that takes account of widening participation, student demand and evidence of employers' needs, but above all the quality of the learning environment. In practice this is a mild intervention in the market but one that prevents HEIs from seeking income with insufficient regard for the student experience and the risk of a significant future fall in demand.

We referred above to e-learning posing a threat as well as an opportunity to HEIs. It is in both contexts that HEFCE (2000b) has launched the e-universities worldwide project. The aim is to develop e-learning markets overseas and for corporate customers. But in doing so it provides universities with development money for the production of new materials and builds up a cadre of experience that can be deployed in the UK. There will be other benefits, including the availability of a sophisticated learning platform and the results of research into e-learning and its impact.

Research

HEFCE allocates nearly £1 billion per year of research money, nearly all on the basis of the RAE, but as we have observed above, if the results have a five-year life then the resources allocated rise to around £5 billion. The degree of selectivity employed in linking assessment grades to money therefore has a profound effect on the finances of a research-intensive university. Even for universities with a more modest research effort the impact on their strategic planning can be very significant. The Funding Council's judgement on balancing the support for world-class research universities on the one hand with the development of a more widely based research capacity on the other becomes an important factor in the financial health of a good many universities. It is important, therefore, that the current debate about a more mission-oriented funding system is resolved fairly quickly because strategic uncertainty is a breeding ground for crises.

Quality assessment and league tables

Quality assessment can directly or indirectly lead to a crisis situation where merger or major restructuring occurs. The risk is greatest when an HEI has a rather narrow range of subjects, as is true for the specialist higher education colleges. Weak assessments by the TTA were the major reasons behind the merger of La Sainte Union College with Southampton University and Bretton Hall College with Leeds University. The role of HEFCE in such cases can involve facilitating discussions and brokering negotiations between merger partners, but the council has had for more than a decade a clear policy of not itself initiating merger discussions, on the grounds that such a top-down intervention is likely to be counterproductive. Mergers, even if forced by external circumstances, do need a wide consensus to be successful. The council is likely to be cognizant of the due diligence processes leading to merger, and once satisfied of the strategic benefit of merger is likely to provide some funding. The negotiations around both the strategy and the level of funding can be quite protracted to ensure that the interests of enrolled students are protected and that the sector as a whole derives maximum benefit from the public funding provided. In the case of Southampton University the merger allowed the development of a new access programme. At Leeds University the merger also provided enhanced access arrangements and allowed an extension of both the education department and work in the creative arts.

A quality report in 1999 had a major impact on Thames Valley University. Interestingly, the report by the QAA was commissioned by the university, but it pointed to a number of weaknesses, which in the ensuing publicity markedly affected recruitment and thus precipitated a financial crisis. This is a very clear illustration of how failings in either quality or management (or both) can in today's highly competitive higher education sector precipitate a financial crisis. Because of the large numbers of universities and colleges and the relative ease of travel the effect of a crisis is likely to be more pronounced in London. With some assistance from HEFCE the university has successfully restructured both its administrative arrangements and its academic programme.

Is there a better approach to formal quality assurance than subject assessment that still protects the student? Broadly speaking, the answer is to provide the student with more information and more up-to-date information. The new quality arrangements (HEFCE 2002b), which replace the cycle of subject teaching assessments in 2003, aim to do that. That is not to say that subject assessments have failed. They were fit for their original purpose and they have raised the standard of teaching and the understanding of the key components of undergraduate learning.

University teaching in 2002 differs considerably from that at the beginning of quality assurance in the early 1990s. Apart from the impact of quality audit and subject assessment, the Institute for Learning and Teaching (see www.ilt.ac.uk) has been created and accredited courses for new lecturers are widespread. HEFCE has a three-pronged strategy: to support institutional strategies and to fund university- and college-wide development activity; to encourage better teaching at the discipline level through the Fund for the Development of Teaching and Learning (HEFCE 2001g); and to highlight the role of individual teachers by means of the Teaching Fellowship Scheme (see www.ntfs.ac.uk), where 20 outstanding teachers are honoured each year.

So the new quality assurance arrangements put the onus on HEIs to publish a flow of data and information about their teaching and learning programme, and on the QAA, through a cycle of institutional reviews, to audit this information and probe weaknesses of provision. By this means the teaching provision of an HEI should be more transparent and the conditions for a critical failure avoided.

There is little evidence on the role of league tables in the student market, although they are certainly eagerly read by members of the university or college senior management team. They do not feature in any Funding Council methodology and do not contain information that is not available elsewhere.

Identification and monitoring of signs of incipient crisis

There are three main ways by which the Funding Council identifies a possible crisis. The first is the longstanding analysis of the financial forecasts and operating plans that universities and colleges provide annually and update at the mid-year. An analysis of these reports gives an indication of the risks facing the sector. In 2001, for example, the main general financial risks were identified as the increasingly diverse range of income sources, increased competition and the reduction of financial flexibility associated with reduced liquidity and higher fixed costs (HEFCE 2001j). In addition there is constraint on the funds necessary both to balance income and expenditure and to reinvest in physical and human capital.

At the level of individual institutions, analysis of these data – which include the current income and expenditure account, future forecasts, the assumptions behind those forecasts and their previous reliability, as well as balance sheet factors such as reserves, borrowing and liquidity – gives an indication of the financial risk. More recently, some of the more general risk factors discussed above have been taken into account but these more subjective elements are examined in the light of a possible impact on future financial performance rather than as a judgement on the way the institution is run.

From these analyses, made by staff who can contribute both a knowledge of the university or college and financial expertise, four categories are identified, which can colloquially be described as: fine; OK but not strong; possible storm clouds in future; and trouble now. HEIs are informed only of their own status and the council is fierce, and successful, in protecting the confidentiality of the occupants of the different categories. For the two lowest categories more frequent reporting of the financial position is required and for the 'in trouble' category a specific action plan will be agreed.

For those institutions with an amber light flashing HEFCE will enter a dialogue aimed at producing a plan which averts any crisis. For institutions judged to have the most severe difficulties – which may number one or as many as six at any one time – the council will require *urgently* an action plan for recovery. This action plan will need to be agreed between the institution and HEFCE and the monitoring will be close, with one-monthly or three-monthly statements required. It is usual for HEFCE to help the university or college to secure external financial advice in drawing up the recovery plan and it may contribute up to 50 per cent of the cost of that advice. But there is no initial assumption of additional financial help or even whether the institution should survive. This robust view is necessary both to emphasize that it is the responsibility of the university or college to find a way round its problems and to indicate to any creditors that HEFCE or the government is not a holding company that will come to the rescue. In practice some assistance is often given to support a recovery plan because it makes financial sense to do so and to ensure that the crisis makes a minimum impact on the current cohort of students.

These arrangements have been demonstrated to work. A number of colleges have merged or been taken over but the core of their work or mission has survived. The great majority of institutions graduate from their crisis state as changed but viable institutions. No university has failed and no college or university limps along with a permanent sense of crisis.

The second source of information comes from audit visits. HEFCE carries out a three-year cycle of visits to institutions, typically with two auditors for a stay of five days. As all institutions are required under their financial memorandum with the Funding Council to have both an internal and an external audit, one could describe the visits as an audit of audits. Even before the Turnbull Report focused attention on the formal analysis of risk the auditors would explore some general areas of risk, and in recent years this has concentrated on governance and management. The findings of the audit report are classified as 'fundamental', 'significant' and 'recommended' to indicate their relative importance, and an agreed action would be required in response to 'fundamental' and 'significant' recommendations. Any findings that would appear to imply a significant risk to the operation of the HEI are reported to the chief executive and his or her senior colleagues.

The work of the council's audit group is overseen by the audit committee of HEFCE, who also agree in general terms its forward programme. The HEFCE audit team seems to be well regarded by institutions and the expectation ought to be that the transfer of good practice conveyed during the visit should fully compensate for the time the HEI spends in preparation. There is, however, some sensitivity around the audit visit and the published advice from HEFCE. The latter is presented as a summary of good practice that it is for the HEI to adopt as a whole or in part on a voluntary basis. Auditors appear, on occasions, to assume that it is more prescriptive than that. The reason probably arises from the fear that the National Audit Office and, more particularly, the Public Accounts Committee see the advisory publications of HEFCE as more of an instruction than is intended.

We should also mention whistle blowing. The council does receive complaints from time to time and these are followed up systematically with the full knowledge and participation of the appropriate HEI staff or governors. The council also requires institutions to report any cases of suspected fraud and the action that is being taken. Such reports, although rare, add to the knowledge of the risks that HEIs face.

The HEFCE audit regime indicates generally sound systems throughout higher education. That is not to suggest that the system is immune from a failure that could develop into a crisis, but it does imply that a rigid cycle of inspection of every HEI every three years is unnecessary. It is logical, as has been proposed, that the frequency of visitation should be linked to the perceived risk and that institutions with a consistently good record of governance and management, risk analysis and financial controls should experience a lighter touch (HEFCE 2002d).

The third and most recent way in which universities and colleges can be engaged in a dialogue about risk arises from the submission of strategic plans and annual operating statements. HEIs are required by the Funding Council to submit strategic plans every three years, with updates in the intervening years. Most HEIs will in any case have submitted plans in component areas in order to apply for specialist funding. Separate strategic statements are likely to exist for all or most institutions in teaching and learning, in widening participation, in research in connection with the RAE and for knowledge transfer with business and the community. Most will have submitted strategic plans for estates and IT and all for human resource management in connection with the government's comprehensive spending review covering the years 2002–4.

The submission of strategic plans to the Funding Council is not new but what makes a difference is the creation of regional consultant positions by HEFCE in 1997. Each consultant has responsibility for all the HEIs in a (government) region and is able to interact much more fully both formally and informally with each university and college. When the strategic plans are seen together with annual operating statements, the financial plans and the latest report from an audit visit, the progress – and risks – can be shared relatively easily, concerns exchanged and further actions planned.

Containment of the threat of a crisis

One can easily argue that good information management is an important step in the containment of a crisis. We have already seen how the Funding Council uses financial information to assess the risk status of institutions. With the more broadly based information described above there is the basis for a constructive dialogue that recognizes both the autonomy of the institution and the wider, albeit indirect, experience of HEFCE. The evidence that this approach is at least partially successful comes from the fact that the number of institutions at some risk of a crisis is if anything lower than in the past despite a more testing environment.

The Funding Council has two more practices that can be important. One arises from the danger inherent in planning based on information that is unreliable. By far the largest part of HEFCE funding is dependent on accurate student data and this will be important for other funding bodies. If student numbers have been exaggerated, or entered in the wrong funding band, there could be serious financial consequences if the error is on a large scale. To minimize this risk HEFCE conducts audits of the data returns made by institutions on a sampling basis.

More important but also more controversial is the financial support given to institutions whose income from the Funding Council suffers a year-on-year decrease. The argument for this income support is that it gives a breathing space for the university or college to plan the necessary actions and to prevent a 'blip' causing a major unravelling of the institution's programme. It also protects the interests of the enrolled students. In practice this means that reductions in HEFCE income have been limited to 1 or 2 per cent. In return for this 'subsidy' institutions have to provide action plans designed to restore the income or to cover a wider restructuring. However, there are some who, privately at least, consider the Funding Council in this instance to be interfering with the normal effects of a market.

Lessons for the future

The lessons to be drawn about managing crises are relatively simple. For universities and colleges risk management matters. And that management of risk has to be both wide-ranging and imaginative with respect to the factors that can influence the development of the institution.

HEFCE has to recognize that many aspects of higher education are indeed governed by the market but some are not. The inability to control the fees of UK and EU undergraduate students prevents the full differentiation of provision, which may bar at least some institutions from developing an optimum role. There is also the fact that research is largely funded as a public good. Funding Councils need to recognize the vulnerability of institutions to rapid changes in the student market and to be ready to provide temporary assistance even in the form of loans to help to smooth the fluctuations as they affect individual universities and colleges. Moreover, although research is concentrated in certain universities, all universities have a strategic interest in research and are affected by changes in research funding policies. Changes in policy therefore need to be accompanied by either appropriate transitional arrangements or a long lead time in the consultation process, but more helpfully by both.

The government too has responsibilities in helping to avoid crises. It has to be sure that its expectations in terms of standards, student numbers and research are matched by realistic levels of funding. If the difference between the two is too large then there is inevitably a greater risk that universities and colleges, in striving to meet government expectations regarding policy and delivery, overreach their capacity.

Finally, there is one dimension of crisis or risk management that has become more critical yet is even today underemphasized. This is leadership. Good leadership obviously matters, but it is not just the leadership of the vice-chancellor or principal. If institutions are to succeed and avoid major problems they will need to be innovative and adaptable, and that requires leadership at all levels. What can universities and colleges do to encourage leadership? At the most elementary level they can recognize the differences between leadership, management and administration and support these functions with resources for staff development. This implies more and better appraisal, formal training, coaching and mentoring. The role of the chair of the governing body and other non-executives impinges in a more subtle way on the leadership of an institution, and now needs the professional attention that is being given by other private and public organizations in the wake of recent well publicized corporate failures. It is important to remember that universities and colleges, though distinctive bodies, have more to learn from other organizations than is often assumed.

11

LEARNING THE LESSONS
Peter Scott

Introduction

The core of this book consists of seven case studies of institutional crises. Two occurred at 'old' universities, although one of these was a new university founded in the 1960s; two at 'new' universities, both in London (which may, or may not, be significant); two at institutes of higher education, which have much in common with the 'new' universities; and one at a further education college (although there have been many more institutional crises in further education, which is underrepresented in this sample). How were these case studies selected? The obvious and immediate answer is that they chose themselves – or, more accurately, they were chosen for us by high-profile media coverage. Cardiff (Shattock 1994), Thames Valley (QAA 1998), Southampton Institute – these are on everyone's A-list of institutional crises. (Although there are a few others on the A-list, such as Huddersfield or Glasgow Caledonian, that are not case studies in this book. Another notable absentee is the Polytechnic, now the University, of North London, presumably a crisis from too long ago and lost in a forgotten world of student protest (Cox *et al.* 1975).)

But this immediately raises a second, and crucial, question: how, and by whom, is an institutional crisis defined? There have been many more near-crises in higher and further education, often involving as difficult and as intractable problems; yet they have not developed into full-blown institutional crises. Recent examples include the problems the University of Cambridge encountered (and the mistakes it made) in introducing its new management information system or South Bank University's need to downsize because of student underrecruitment. These examples of near-crises could easily be multiplied. Many, perhaps most, universities and colleges regularly experience near-crises; indeed, crisis management is both familiar and frequent (and inevitable?) in an underfunded and overregulated system.

One definition of full-blown crises is that they occur when institutional problems cannot be resolved without external intervention – a *deus ex machina* in the form of an imposed 'company doctor', a new vice-chancellor (or principal) or a forced merger. In contrast, near-crises are resolved through internal action (perhaps with a little help from outside). A second definition is that in the case of the former a critical mass of bad publicity sets off a chain reaction of even more damaging consequences, while in the case of the latter the bad publicity remains sub-critical and this chain reaction of damaging consequences is avoided. A third definition of a full-blown crisis is that it is often a combination of deep-rooted structural problems – inefficient management systems or inappropriate institutional positioning – and of contingent circumstances that exacerbate these problems – an overambitious (or ineffective) chief executive, divisions within the senior management team, poor industrial relations or a whiff of impropriety or scandal. Near-crises, on the other hand, may be characterized by one or the other. In other words, institutions can be either bad or mad but not both.

The A-list of institutional crises tends to display all three characteristics: an eventual need for high-profile external intervention; a chain reaction of bad publicity; and a combination of structural problems and contingent factors. Full-blown institutional crises are exceptional events, but also perhaps the peak of a much larger iceberg. Such crises are exceptional, first, because they are remarkably rare and, second, because they tend to be produced by an equally remarkable (and rare) combination of bad management and bad luck. But they are also the peak of an iceberg in the sense that many of the contributory factors – such as inadequate funding, 'overtrading', inefficient and unreliable systems, weak management and lack of strategic direction – are present, to a greater or lesser degree, in many institutions. So, while recognizing that such crises are rare events (which reflects well on the overall standard of management in higher and further education), their lessons are relevant to the sector as a whole.

The dog that did not bark

The most remarkable characteristic of institutional crises is their infrequency. Over the past two decades no HEI has failed financially and none has closed, although a few have come perilously close (and might even have been, technically, insolvent) and a small number have been forced to merge with more robust neighbours. The large majority of universities and colleges funded by the Higher Education Funding Council for England (HEFCE) has remained in the council's highest 'financial health' category, and the number on HEFCE's worry list has rarely gone into double figures. The position in Scotland and Wales has been equally resilient. During that period the only merger between universities that could be attributed to a full-blown institutional crisis (as opposed to mergers designed to produce strategic advantage) was between the then University College Cardiff and the University of Wales Institute of Science and Technology, one of the case studies in this book. The other involuntary mergers were between smaller colleges of higher education that had been overwhelmed by crises, whether financial or managerial, and larger universities. In further education the story has been similar, which is perhaps even more remarkable in the light of the 'shock treatment' of incorporation in 1992, when colleges ceased to be maintained (and their institutional integrity guaranteed) by local education authorities. Although there have been frequent examples of crises or scandals (often highlighted in *Private Eye*'s 'Rotten Principals' column), the degree of institutional rationalization in the sector has been limited.

The infrequency of institutional crises is remarkable for four reasons. The first is that throughout this period both higher and further education have been both seriously underfunded and required to deliver substantial 'efficiency gains'. In higher education, unit costs have been reduced by more than a third in little more than a decade; partly, it must be admitted, as a result of the enthusiasm of institutions for recruiting marginally funded students (in the – naive? – expectation that these additional students would one day attract full funding), but mainly because year-on-year 'efficiency gains' have been imposed on the sector by successive governments. In further education many colleges have been faced with the need for 'migration'; in other words, regression to sector-wide budget norms. Initially the potential impact of funding levels on institutional viability was carefully monitored by the Further Education Funding Council (FEFC), but it is not clear that the Learning and Skills Council, which has replaced the FEFC, has the same concern (or competence?). The stresses and strains of these improvements in 'efficiency', unaccompanied it should be remembered by any corresponding productivity shift in the use of academic labour (despite the – false? – promises of information technology), on staff and systems have gone largely unanalysed, or even unacknowledged. But, almost certainly, these pressures increased the propensity for institutional breakdown.

The second reason is that both higher and further education institutions have had to enter more problematical student markets, either in the sense that conventional demand has been unreliable, static or even declining, or in the sense that they now recruit students with more complex (and, potentially, more costly) learning needs. Both factors are important. Between the mid-1980s and mid-1990s student demand was buoyant. But since the late 1990s, despite the Labour government's target of 50 per cent participation in higher education by the end of the present decade (by 30-year-olds and younger), the system has moved closer to steady state – at any rate, as measured by UCAS (2002) applications. Although HEFCE has attempted to nudge institutions into espousing growth by awarding them additional student numbers (and, of course, additional funding), barely half of these ASNs have represented genuine growth; the rest have simply contributed to the 'churning' of student numbers as more popular institutions have benefited at the expense of the less popular (HEFCE 2001h). As a result, a significant number of institutions has experienced persistent difficulties in recruiting their contract student numbers, and suffered clawback of their grants. The position in further education has been more volatile. But here too targets have been undershot, with serious consequences for some colleges.

In higher education most, but not all, of the institutions with recruitment difficulties have been 'new' universities or larger colleges (and institutes) of higher education, which are also the institutions with the highest proportions of non-traditional students who are, potentially, more expensive because they demand, and deserve, more elaborate support than students from more conventional backgrounds. As a result these institutions have been doubly disadvantaged. Not only have they been most vulnerable to clawback because of underrecruitment, they have also not been adequately compensated for the additional cost of teaching non-traditional students. Again, chronic underrecruitment and the higher costs of teaching non-traditional students will have increased the likelihood of institutional crises. At the very least they have reduced the margin for error, or safety cushion, enjoyed by such institutions. There is no immediate sign that conditions are likely to improve in terms of overall demand; nor is there much prospect that these additional costs are likely to be fully reflected in Funding Council grants to institutions. Instead, there is evidence that, as potential students recognize that the steady state has enhanced their ability to pick and choose between institutions, polarization between high-demand and low-demand institutions is increasing. As a result, high-demand institutions have little fear of clawback for underrecruitment, and they predominantly recruit more conventional students who are cheaper to teach (and these institutions are also likely to enjoy substantial research funding).

The third reason is that both higher and further education have been subject to an increasing burden of regulation – in the excellent cause of better accountability and improved efficiency, of course. Certainly some aspect of this regulation has benefited institutions by leading to improvements in their management and upgrading of their systems, and consequently reduced the likelihood of institutional crises. Similarly, increasing surveillance by HEFCE and similar agencies, however intrusive, has provided early warning of potential institutional failures. But there are other aspects of increasing regulation that may have had the opposite effect. One has been the growing influence of performance measurement, compounded by the fact that most performance criteria have been – perhaps inevitably – conservative rather than innovative. For example, institutions with higher proportions of non-traditional students have been punished for also having higher non-continuation rates (if only indirectly, because they have had to increase their initial intakes to produce sufficient fundable students). Another has been the financial and administrative burden of increasing regulation, which may have been particularly heavy for smaller institutions (already at greater risk of institutional breakdown because of their more limited management capacity and less sophisticated management systems). The transactional and frictional costs of regulation have rarely been accounted for properly.

A final, and perhaps the most significant, example of the negative impact of regulation was the development of deliberately high-profile assessment systems for teaching and research (Scott 2000; Shore and Wright 2000). In at least two of the case study institutions an important trigger of the crisis was criticism of their academic standards by the Quality Assurance Agency (QAA) following an unsatisfactory audit or assessment. This criticism produced a chain reaction of adverse criticism, which led to an internal collapse of morale and an external collapse of competitiveness and made an institutional crisis all but inevitable. In both cases this action may well have been justified. There is certainly no justification for concealing serious academic weaknesses from potential students and graduate employers. But the overall impact of teaching and research assessment, although less dramatic, may be more serious. Such assessments exercise a significant influence over the market position of institutions. A run of disappointing results, whether in individual subject reviews (and, no doubt, the whole-institution audits that will succeed them) or the Research Assessment Exercise (RAE), reduces institutional competitiveness in terms of the capacity to recruit students (home and international, undergraduate and postgraduate) or to attract additional research funding. As a result, institutions may become more vulnerable to crises.

A fourth reason is the organizational ethos of most institutions, at any rate in higher education. Despite talk of the advance of 'managerialism' and the substantial investment in the development of more effective leadership and better management, universities and colleges continue to be deeply influenced by collegial values (Pritchard 2000). Typically they are loosely coupled low-compliance, high-consensus organizations. This description is not intended to be critical. The essence of universities in particular is that real authority, academic authority rooted in disciplinary and professional cultures, must be widely distributed, because this is a precondition of creativity and innovation, quality and standards. Universities cannot be run as centralized 'command' bureaucracies. Two consequences flow from this. First, HEIs, although not inherently unmanageable, must be intuitively and sensitively managed. Effective leadership demands political skills of persuasion, authentic role-modelling and charismatic, even visionary, qualities, because institutions far more often need re-enchantment than re-engineering (or, rather, they may need both, but in that order) (Bargh *et al.* 2000). But such a leadership style is not easy to maintain when an institution is under stress – and decisions, perhaps abrupt and arbitrary, are needed. Second (and conversely), some institutional crises have been provoked by the perceived failure of their leaders to stay true to core institutional values, which may be why the personality of the vice-chancellor is so often a key element in the story. Apart from high-profile negative publicity, such as critical QAA reports, conflict between organizational ethos and managerial ambition has been the most important trigger for institutional crises.

All four of these reasons – underfunding, faltering (or novel) student demand, increasing regulation and the persistence of collegiality – would tend to suggest that higher (and, to a lesser extent, further) education institutions should be especially vulnerable to crises. In fact, the reverse appears to be true. Full-blown crises have been rare. There are almost no examples of true 'market failure', as opposed to reckless management. Why? As Sherlock Holmes remarked in *Silver Blaze*, the fact that 'the dog did nothing in the nighttime' may be in itself remarkable. One possible answer is that, against all the odds, HEIs are generally well managed. The Treasury, the Scottish Executive, the Department for Education and Skills (DfES) and other departments of state, with HEFCE and the other Funding

Councils taking their cue from their political masters, are unlikely to be convinced. Improving leadership and management in higher education is seen as an urgent priority. Another possible answer is that, despite the adverse factors that have just been described, crises arise out of special circumstances peculiar to individual institutions rather than from generic conditions such as underfunding and overregulation. This is certainly true, in the limited sense that all institutional crises are in themselves unique episodes; but this does not mean that underlying structural causes can be entirely discounted. Before any firm conclusion could be reached a more comprehensive analysis not only of these full-blown crises but also of the much greater number of near-crises would need to be undertaken.

A third possible answer is that university and college managers have become highly adept at managing resource deficiency, institutional austerity and, in the worst cases, decline. But if this is true it has come at a cost – or two costs. First, both higher and further education institutions are overtrading, in the sense that almost none is making adequate provision for maintaining and renewing its capital (physical and human) and few are making adequate provision for reinvestment in innovation. This cannot go on for ever, as the Treasury has been convinced in the case of research. Second, the infrequency of crises may suggest that institutions have become too risk-averse. Creativity may be being curbed because it is too dangerous. Furthermore, this caution may be compounded by a false view of the consequences of competition in higher and further education, namely the desire of institutions to find distinctive niches or, at the very least, to concentrate on their strengths and eliminate their weaknesses – and, consequently, to stimulate novelty. In the market economy one way to assess the degree of innovation in a particular sector is to count the market failures. The closer one is to the cutting edge of change, the more risks need to be taken. Higher education does not score well in this respect, although further education's 'performance' is a little better.

Common features

Two questions need to be asked about the seven case studies described in this book and other high-profile institutional crises. First, is it possible to discern any pattern in the types, or sizes, of institution that appear to be most at risk? Second, are there common features that all, or most of, these crises exhibit – bearing in mind, of course, that full-blown crises like these are all special cases?

The first question is difficult to answer because the number of case studies is so small. The three main categories of higher education institution – 'old' universities, 'new' universities and colleges of higher education – are all represented. This tends to support the argument that full-blown crises are random events. But on closer examination a more interesting picture emerges. First, the non-university institutions are overrepresented. This probably reflects both their smaller size and their lower position in the hierarchy of institutional esteem. The former is likely to have influenced the calibre of their administrative and support staff (and of their managers?) and the sophistication of their management information systems, while the latter is likely to have influenced the solidity of their resource base. Second, most were small or medium-sized – at any rate, in comparison with other institutions of their type. Although both London Guildhall and Thames Valley were substantial institutions, both were below-average in size among 'new' universities. Cardiff was, then, a pocket-sized civic university, while Lancaster was among the smaller of the new universities established in the 1960s. Southampton Institute was a giant in its own class, colleges of higher education, but well below the average for higher education as a whole.

Third, if a 'binary' taxonomy is applied, the majority of the crises occurred outside the 'old' university sector. This is remarkable in the sense that it is generally believed that executive management has been more fully developed in the 'new' universities and colleges, which should have made full-blown crises easier to avoid; less remarkable perhaps in the sense that 'old' universities still typically enjoy a larger 'comfort zone' in which mistakes can be made without full-blown crises developing (and their organizational cultures, which place greater emphasis on collegiality, may make them more reluctant to 'wash their dirty linen in public'). Finally, the two crises in the 'old' universities do seem to be special cases. Both occurred some time in the past; Cardiff dates back to the days of the University Grants Committee, which was abolished 15 years ago. One – Cardiff again – was characterized by a high degree of personal idiosyncrasy. As has already been noted, the other – Lancaster – was a comparatively small university, which, moreover, was geographically remote. It is difficult to escape the conclusion that neither exhibited features that could be easily associated with 'old' universities as a group, although this sector has had its fair share of near-crises. The sample-of-one from further education makes it impossible to draw any valid conclusions.

The second question – are there common features among these case studies of institutional crises? – is also difficult to answer, for the same reasons. The sample of seven crises is small, and skewed. Full-blown crises are, by definition, atypical in the sense that special factors tend to overwhelm structural factors. An analysis of near-crises might be more fruitful in terms of exposing generic causal factors. Nevertheless, it is possible to identify four arenas of crisis. The first is structural weakness: for example, in terms of inadequate and/or inappropriate estate or of inadequate financial reserves. The second is ineffective management systems, whether student records or budgetary controls. The third is lack of strategic direction, leading either to a failure to position the institution sensibly or to the pursuit of unrealizable ambitions. The fourth is an omnibus arena in which people are the key players: chief executives, other senior managers, governing bodies, administrative and support staff, academic staff (perhaps in the role of the 'opposition').

Structural weakness

The first cause for the development of crises is the underlying weakness of the institution. This weakness typically takes one (or both) of two forms: poor estate, typically scattered over a number of sites, and a lack of adequate reserves. London Guildhall is a good example of the former. Although the institution experienced other difficulties, its fundamental problem was that it was housed in a number of buildings, most of which were on expensive short-term leases and few of which were fit for purpose. At Thames Valley, although the triggers for the immediate crisis were a highly critical QAA report and serious staff discontent, an important background cause was the university's struggle to reconfigure campuses at Ealing in West London and at Slough. Of course, many other institutions – including nearly all the 'new' universities and many colleges of higher education and further education colleges – have had to operate in buildings designed for very different activities (even when they were designed with educational use in mind, which was not always the case) and on poorly configured campuses. But this is clearly an important factor in predisposing an institution to crisis. The running costs of such estate are high; its configuration often inhibits sensible institutional development (or encourages senior managers to attempt overambitious restructuring, as seems to have been the case at the University of Western Sydney in Australia); and institutions are inevitably tempted to adopt 'big bang' solutions to escape these constraints (a risky enterprise that can all too easily lead to financial disaster).

This leads on to the second weakness, the lack of adequate reserves, which is often associated with poor estates. As a result, the poorest universities and colleges have been tempted to take the biggest risks in order to secure more optimal institutional configurations. But it was not simply a question of heightened financial risk; such large-scale projects often demanded highly developed project management skills, which were (are?) comparatively rare in higher education. By the 1980s and 1990s such projects also had to be developed in a more exposed, and commercial, environment; earlier large-scale developments, such as the building of the new universities in the 1960s, were fully funded by the state. Typically they had to be funded through complex financing deals, sometimes involving disposal of existing property, which often significantly increased the burden of institutional debt. Sometimes inappropriate deals were struck, as appears to have been the case at Lancaster. If these projects went wrong, their failure could easily be attributed to the vanity (megalomania, even) of the vice-chancellor or principal. Even if they went right, the consequent debt burden could be represented as inhibiting 'core' academic development. Moreover, as appears to have been the situation with several of the case studies, indebted institutions with inadequate reserves were heavily dependent on student recruitment (home or international) to maintain their income levels. A downturn in recruitment, and consequential loss of income, could quickly produce a financial crisis.

Ineffective systems

Several of the case study institutions appear to have had ineffective management information systems. This also seems to have been a feature of many of the much more numerous near-crises (HEFCE 1998). For example, two decades ago the University of Edinburgh ran into financial difficulties because its personnel system did not accurately record its payroll costs; more recently some 'new' universities have been penalized for overreporting their student numbers. Just as on occasions senior managers in institutions vulnerable to developing crises lacked the project management skills needed to implement successfully their large-scale restructuring and/or development plans, so administrative and support staff seem to have lacked the system tools required for the routine management of institutional processes – and, crucially, to be able to make reliable reports to senior managers. Often income seems to have been overestimated, while costs were understated. When the true position became known, it was sometimes too late to take sensible and measured corrective action – and a full-blown crisis arose unannounced.

The proximate cause, of course, was a failure to invest in the necessary management information systems. There seem to have been three main substantive causes. The first was a failure on the part of senior management to recognize the importance of reliable and responsive systems, perhaps out of a mistaken belief in the virtues of intuitive, individualistic, even charismatic management styles. The second was a lack of the financial resources and/or good practice advice needed to secure and develop such systems: in the case of some, mainly smaller, institutions an absolute lack; in the case of others a comparative lack (in other words, the failure to give such investment a sufficiently high priority, which is also linked to the first cause). The third substantive cause was a failure to appreciate the synergies between effective management systems – and, of course, robust performance measures – and organizational development. It has been argued that universities were once held together by a common academic culture and that now they are held together by the standardized processes required by modern management systems. This argument is probably flawed on two counts: first, because the common academic culture was almost certainly a myth; second, because values are not necessarily subordinated to systems. Institutions have a choice: their mission and values can be driven by their management systems (and performance indicators), or their management systems can be driven by their mission and values. But values and systems are inextricably linked.

Strategic direction

A third arena from which institutional crises often seem to have arisen is a lack of clarity about strategic direction. Some of the case study institutions were continuing to behave in ways, academic and financial, that were no longer sensible (or perhaps feasible) under new conditions. Cardiff might have fallen into that category until it was called to account by the UGC, although the waywardness of its pre-crisis trajectory makes it difficult to be sure. Southampton Institute attempted to grow in size, although this growth eventually turned out to be unsustainable, in order to be able to aspire to polytechnic status, even after the rules of that particular game had been changed and the polytechnics absorbed into the university sector. Others pursued overambitious strategies. For example, Thames Valley appears to have seen its investment in computer-based learning systems as potentially creating a 'new economy' in higher education that would displace the 'old economy' of conventional face-to-face teaching and library-based learning. Lancaster seems to have believed that, by funding new buildings through its bond issue, it could break through into a new (and higher) league of university players – perhaps lured on by the successful example of Warwick, but taking too little account of their different circumstances.

However, the institutions that went on to develop full-blown crises were not unique in this respect. Many other institutions followed anachronistic courses or pursued overambitious strategies. What was special about the case study institutions that predisposed them to crisis? One answer is that, while other institutions got it wrong, they got it very wrong. In other words, the crucial difference was a matter of degree. Institutions that developed crises were often pursuing strategies that were clearly unsustainable, given their overall position in the higher (or further) education market place. A second answer is that in some cases there appears to have been an especially high degree of normative dissonance: the gap between existing values and practice and what was perceived to be the self-indulgent (and even vainglorious) ambitions of senior managers had become a gulf. A third answer may be that at-risk institutions, typically 'new' universities and colleges of higher education, were characterized by a dangerous combination of strong (and unaccountable and anti-collegial?) executive management and fuzziness of mission, particularly after the abandonment of the binary system in 1992. There was both the scope and the incentive to develop 'grand plans'. A fourth reason may simply be that at-risk institutions had less room for manoeuvre, in terms of funding and reputation; they had fewer options and less opportunity to recover from any mistakes.

People and personalities

The fourth arena in which institutional crises arose was the one that has received the most (perhaps too much) emphasis: people and personalities. That there might have been too much emphasis is because full-blown crises inevitably sharpen personal antagonisms and create battle lines. Once this polarization has taken place it is too easy to blame individuals (the overmighty vice-chancellor or his overcompliant senior management colleagues) or groups (the irresponsible professors or the Luddite trade unionists). But, on occasions, this may be to put the cart before the horse. If no crisis had arisen, or it had been contained, there might have been no breakdown in personal relationships – even if these relationships had previously been unhappy. Only in three of the case studies can even a plausible case be made for arguing that the trigger for the crisis was the unreasonable behaviour of senior managers. Of course, this does

not mean that, once a crisis has unfolded and personal relationships have deteriorated, no resolution is possible without certain
individuals being made responsible, and being expected to carry the
consequences.

However, while we must bear this note of caution in mind, there
were a number of features that most full-blown crises had in common. The first was a failure of governance. It is remarkable how small
a part was played by the council or governing body in most of the
case studies. Typically theirs was a 'bit' part in the unfolding drama.
Even in the aftermath of the crisis, council or governing body
members were rarely called to personal account; it seemed to be taken
for granted that their powers to intervene had been limited. This
has certainly been the case in higher education; in further education
governing bodies have tended to take a more activist role, although
not always with happy results. An important cause of their impotence
seemed to have been their dominance by the senior management,
particularly in the context of information flows (Bargh *et al.* 1996).
Too often they were 'in the pockets' of the management. But in some
cases senior council or governing body members appear to have
believed that it was their responsibility to aid and abet the ambitions
of senior management, and effectively abandoned their fiduciary
responsibilities.

A second feature in common was a failure of leadership. In some
cases too much seems to have been demanded of vice-chancellors and
principals in increasingly difficult circumstances, given their training
for these demanding roles (little or none), their management com-
petences and their previous experience (almost entirely within the
academic system). Their response was adventurism, devising grand
plans that had little basis in reality, or avoidance, a reluctance to take
timely decisions, or a combination of both. A third feature was a
breakdown of collegiality, either within the narrow bounds of the
senior management team or in the institution more widely. In some
cases this was accompanied by a lack of transparency, in others by the
growth of a hectoring style of communication. As a result a healthy
system of checks and balances broke down, disagreements with the
chief executive were regarded as disloyalty and dissent within
the broader institutional community was treated as rebellion. The
'dissidents' then felt they had no choice but to resort to 'whistle-
blowing', and the ensuing negative publicity then triggered a full-
blown crisis.

It is important to emphasize that, although these four arenas can be
identified as giving rise to the factors predisposing institutions to
developing full-blown crises, it was typically a combination of factors,
and the relationship between them, that actually triggered the crises

described in the case studies. In none of the case studies were all four present in full strength. None of these institutions was all bad. The events at Cardiff, for example, can largely be attributed to the instability of the senior management team – and, in particular, the personality of the principal – and its impact on relationships between the institution and external agencies, principally the UGC. Although the crisis did have a financial dimension, its scale was modest by later standards. Cardiff University's current success suggests that the essential underlying strengths of the institution had not been impaired as much as the immediate crisis implied. At the other end of the scale, the problems facing London Guildhall were intractable and would have daunted the most decisive management. The merger between London Guildhall and the University of North London to form London Metropolitan University suggests that it was eventually accepted that no stable or long-term resolution was possible within the compass of the existing institution. The other case study institutions lie along this spectrum between crises created by personalities and crises rooted in structural deficiencies.

Lessons for the future

Successful strategies for avoiding crises are the flip-sides of the factors that predispose institutions to succumb to full-blown crises in the first place. First, institutions should ensure they possess easy-to-manage, economical and fit-for-purpose estate, and, of course, adequate reserves to provide a 'comfort zone' if things do not go according to plan. Sadly not all institutions are in this fortunate position, and the position with regard to aggregate reserves is worsening. In effect, higher education is 'running on empty'. The total surpluses generated by universities and colleges of higher education in England are a fraction of 1 per cent of turnover, and most of that is 'funny money' generated by exceptional items (notably asset disposals) (HEFCE 2001j). Second, institutions should provide themselves with state-of-the-art management information systems, so that senior managers cannot remain under any illusions about the true state of their 'business'. Here the picture is a little brighter: substantial investments have been made in upgrading systems in higher education in recent years. Third, institutions should be realistic about their actual (and achievable) position within the higher education market place. If only! As a result of the frenetic competition generated by the RAE at least 25 universities have set themselves the goal of being in the top ten research universities next time round, while the financial forecasts of a number of students assume student growth that is belied by past performance. Finally, institutions should ensure that governing bodies take their fiduciary responsibilities seriously, that vice-chancellors and principals are both painstaking managers and visionary leaders, that senior managers operate as a harmonious team and that all staff are fully engaged. Again, if only! All institutions are prey to dissent and, therefore, potentially to dissension. This is how it should be. Creativity, risk-taking, innovation and crisis are bundled together more closely than is often imagined.

However, there are four levels at which action can be taken to minimize the likelihood of full-blown institutional crises:

- *Government.* The DfES and HEFCE, and sister ministries and agencies in Scotland and Wales, must recognize that a major risk factor is the underfunding of higher and further education, and that recent policy initiatives, such as the decision to require students to make a contribution to the cost of their tuition, have increased the pressure on institutional management without materially increasing the resources. In other words, they have increased the pain without taking any of the strain. A decision to 'allow' institutions to charge so-called top-up fees would compound these difficulties. Moreover, the balkanization of funding into segmented initiatives, designed to 'steer' the system without engaging in top-down planning and to enhance accountability ('something for something'), is also a risk factor because it increases the burden on institutions, while reducing their flexibility.
- *Governing bodies.* Courts, councils and governing bodies should concentrate on their own job – governance (i.e. reviewing performance, testing assumptions, scrutinizing policies) – instead of seeking either to share in or to take over the management of institutions. If they become too close to management, they not only share in its successes but become compromised by its failures. Instead they need to preserve a certain distance, and, in addition to their formal responsibilities, act as 'critical friends'. But to be able to do this, governing bodies need to be supported by more independent secretariats. Governing bodies should strive to be representative, both externally, by reflecting the diversity of the communities their institutions serve, and internally, by encouraging a pluralism of perspectives. The size of governing bodies, so often seen as the key to their effectiveness, is a secondary issue.
- *Senior managers.* Vice-chancellors and principals should see themselves predominantly as academic leaders and *primi inter pares*, not as chief executives with line managers reporting to them. The responsibilities of leadership should be emphasized, not its powers

and privileges. The cult of 'managerialism' should be actively discouraged, as antithetical to effective leadership. There may be advantages in rotating members of the senior management team to reduce the likelihood of cliques and cabals, provided this does not compromise professional competence. The process of decision-making should be fully transparent. The widest possible consultation should take place on key decisions, inside and outside institutions. But more senior managers should receive more systematic preparation for their roles and, as an even higher priority, continuing support and (where appropriate) training.

- *Management systems.* Higher and further education institutions are highly complex organizations, offering hundreds (perhaps thousands) of different 'products' to their 'customers', and these 'products' are constantly changing as a result of new research advances, shifting student demand and the emergence of new economic, social and cultural environments. Yet, too often, their management systems are more primitive than those possessed by less complex organizations in the private sector (or elsewhere in the public sector). There needs to be a step-change in universities and colleges to enable them to become similarly data-rich institutions. Recent developments in information and communication technologies have also substantially reduced the cost and enhanced the functionality of management systems; these developments have also encouraged convergence and increased accessibility. As a result, distinctions between 'information' tools and 'control' systems are breaking down.

Finally, how can crises be managed once they have occurred, as they inevitably will? In the case studies presented in this book the answer was nearly always external intervention – to sort out the books, depose discredited management, clear the air and enable institutions to make a new start. In some cases intervention was limited, perhaps confined to a hard-hitting enquiry what then provided the catalyst for change by established institutional organs. In other cases intervention was more far-reaching: the permanent replacement of institutional leaders. The latter approach is now the standard response in the wider public sector. New managers are drafted in to run 'failing' hospitals; 'super-heads' are appointed to turn round 'failing' schools. However, this approach is built on the assumption that the root cause is confined to management, rather than market, failure. With full-blown crises this is typically the case – or, to be more accurate, it is management failure, often compounded by personality conflicts, that tips the balance. With near-crises, which are much more numerous (and may even be endemic), the position is often less straightforward: sometimes it is easy to remedy obvious deficiencies in management competence, but in other cases deep-rooted structural problems remain that can be addressed only over a long haul. A strategy for managing crises in higher education needs to be sufficiently sensitive to address both eventualities: short, sharp external intervention in the case of full-blown crises for certain; but also careful analyses, and more measured action plans, to tackle deep-rooted and intractable problems.

REFERENCES

Albrighton, F. and Thomas, J. (2001) *Managing External Relations*. Buckingham: Open University Press.

Allen, P. C. (1980) *Stanford*. Stanford, CA: Stanford Historical Society.

Atkinson, D. (2002) *College Turnaround: Guidance on Colleges in Recovery*. London: Learning and Skills Development Agency.

The Australian (2001a) Along the bumpy road to self-reliance, *The Australian*, 14 November, 32–3.

The Australian (2001b) Difference in recall, *The Australian*, 21 November, 34.

Bain, A. (1993) *Private Sector Funding in Higher Education*. London: Higher Education Funding Council for England.

Balchin, W. G. V. (1959) The university expansion in Great Britain, *New Scientist*, 12 March.

Bargh, C., Bocock, J., Scott, P. and Smith, D. (1996) *Governing Universities: Changing the Culture?* Buckingham: Open University Press.

Bargh, C., Bocock, J., Scott, P. and Smith, D. (2000) *University Leadership: The Role of the Chief Executive*. Buckingham: Open University Press.

Barnett, R. (2000) *Realizing the University in an age of supercomplexity*. Buckingham: Open University Press.

Becher, T. and Kogan, M. (1992) *Process and Structure in Higher Education*. London: Routledge.

Brown, R. (2001a) The governance of the new universities: do we need to think again?, *Perspectives*, 5(1), 42–7.

Brown, R. (2001b) Accountability in higher education: the case for a higher education audit commission, *Higher Education Review*, 33(2), 5–20.

Brown, R. (2002) Quality assurance: past, present and future. Keynote speech delivered at the AUA Conference, University of Southampton, 8 April.

Cabinet Office (2002) *Higher Education: Easing the Burden*. London: The Stationery Office.

Campus Review (2002) UWS targets research with bold reforms, *Campus Review*, 12(1), 1.

Clark, B. R. (1998) *Creating Entrepreneurial Universities: Organizational Pathways of Transformation*. Paris: Elsevier Science.

Clark, B. R. (2001) The entrepreneurial university: new foundations for collegiality, autonomy, and achievement, *Higher Education Management*, 13(2), 9–24.

Considine, M. and Marginson, S. (2000) *The Enterprise University: Power, Governance and Reinvention in Australia*. Cambridge: Cambridge University Press.

Cox, C., Jacka, K. and Marks, J. (1975) *The Rape of Reason: The Corruption of the Polytechnic of North London*. Enfield: Churchill Press.

Crickhowell, N. (1999) *Westminster, Wales and Water*. Cardiff: University of Wales Press.

Department of Education and Science (1987) *Higher Education: Meeting the Challenge*, Cmnd 114. London: HMSO.

Department of Education and Science (1991) *Higher Education: A New Framework*, Cmnd 1541. London: HMSO.

Department for Education and Skills (2001) *Education and Skills: Delivering Results – A Strategy to 2006*. London: DfES Publications.

Department for Trade and Industry (2000) *Excellence and Opportunity: A Science and Innovation Policy for the Twenty-first Century*. London: DTI.

Dixon, S. and Leevers, S. (1999) *More and Better for Less: A Three Card Trick*. London: Further Education Development Agency.

Duke, C. (2000) Beyond 'delayering': process, structure and boundaries, *Higher Education Management*, 12(1), 7–22.

Duke, C. (2001a) Networks and managerialism: field-testing competing paradigms, *Journal of Higher Education Policy and Management*, 23(1), 103–18.

Duke, C. (2001b) Cultural change and the machinery of management, *Higher Education Management*, 13(3), 31–44.

Duke, C. (2002) *Managing the Learning University*. Buckingham: Society for Research into Higher Education and Open University Press.

Dykes, D. (1992) *The University College of Swansea: An Illustrated History*. Bath: Allan Sutton.

Further Education Funding Council (1993) *Units of Funding*, Circular 93/09. Coventry: FEFC.

Further Education Funding Council (2001a) *Using Management Information to Raise Standards*. Coventry: FEFC.

Further Education Funding Council (2001b) *Lambeth College: Report from the Inspectorate*. Coventry: FEFC.

Goodwin, J. and Cunningham, V. (2001) *Cardiff University: A Celebration*. Cardiff: Cardiff University.

Gottschalk, J. (2002) *Crisis Management*. Oxford: Capstone Publications.

Hall, G. (1996) *The Hall Report*. Southampton: Southampton Institute.

Harman, G. and Robertson-Cuninghame, R. (eds) (1995) *The Network UNE Experience. Reflections on the Amalgamated University of New England 1989–1993*. Armidale: UNE.

Harvard Business Review on Crisis Management (2000) New York: Harvard Business School Press

Harvard Business Review on Turnarounds (2001) New York: Harvard Business School Press.

Higher Education Funding Council for England (1998) *Information Systems and Technology Management: Value for Money Study (National Report)*. Bristol: HEFCE (98/42).

Higher Education Funding Council for England (1999a) *Chinese Studies*. Bristol: HEFCE (99/35).

Higher Education Funding Council for England (1999b) *Teaching Quality Enhancement Fund: Funding Arrangements*. Bristol: HEFCE (99/48).

Higher Education Funding Council for England (2000a) *Model Financial Memorandum between HEFCE and Institutions*. Bristol: HEFCE (00/25).

Higher Education Funding Council for England (2000b) *e-University Project: Business Model*. Bristol: HEFCE (00/43).

Higher Education Funding Council for England (2001a) *Rewarding and Developing Staffing Higher Education*. Bristol: HEFCE (01/16).

Higher Education Funding Council for England (2001b) *Risk Management: A Briefing for Governors and Senior Managers*. Bristol: HEFCE (01/24).

Higher Education Funding Council for England (2001c) *The Management of Student Administration: A Guide to Good Practice*. Bristol: HEFCE (01/27).

Higher Education Funding Council for England (2001d) *Risk Management: A Guide to Good Practice for Higher Education Institutions*. Bristol: HEFCE (01/28).

Higher Education Funding Council for England (2001e) *Strategies for Learning and Teaching: A Guide to Good Practice*. Bristol: HEFCE (01/37).

Higher Education Funding Council for England (2001f) *Additional Student Places and Funds 2002–3: Invitation to Bid*. Bristol: HEFCE (01/54).

Higher Education Funding Council for England (2001g) *FDTL Phase Four*. Bristol: HEFCE (01/60).

Higher Education Funding Council for England (2001h) *Supply and Demand in Higher Education*. Bristol: HEFCE (01/62).

Higher Education Funding Council for England (2001i) *Performance Indicators in Higher Education in the UK*. Bristol: HEFCE (01/69).

Higher Education Funding Council for England (2001j) *Analysis of Corporate Plans, Outcomes of 2001 Financial Forecasts and Annual Operating Statements*. Bristol: HEFCE (01/71).

Higher Education Funding Council for England (2002a) *Science Research Investment Fund: Invitation to Apply for Funding*. Bristol: HEFCE (02/11).

Higher Education Funding Council for England (2002b) *Information on Quality and Standards in Higher Education: Final Report of the Task Group*. Bristol: HEFCE (02/15).

Higher Education Funding Council for England (2002c) *Corporate Plan 2002–7*. Bristol: HEFCE (02/20).

Higher Education Funding Council for England (2002d) *Audit Code of Practice*. Bristol: HEFCE (02/26).

Institute of Chartered Accountants in England and Wales (1999) *The Turnbull Report. Internal Control: Guidance for Directors on the Combined Code*. London: ICAEW.

Jarman, A. and Kouzmin, A. (1990) Decision pathways from crisis, *Contemporary Crisis*, 14, 399–433.

Jay, R. (2001) *Fast Thinking Crisis*. London: Pearson Professional.

Kanter, R. M. (1983) *The Change Masters*. London: Unwin.

Kaplin, W. and Lee, B. (1995) *The Law of Higher Education*. New York: Jossey-Bass.

Kay, J. (1993) *Foundations of Corporate Success*. Oxford: Open University Press.

Keller, G. (1983) *Academic Strategy: The Management Revolution in American Higher Education*. Baltimore: Johns Hopkins University Press.

Kennedy, H. (1997) *Learning Works*. Coventry: FEFC.

Kets de Vries, M. and Miller, D. (1984) *The Neurotic Organization*. San Francisco: Jossey-Bass.

Korac-Kakabadse, A., Korac-Kakabadse, N. and Kouzmin, A. (1998) Negotiating consultant links with the top team: transacting meaning and obligations or executive failure through excessive outsourcing?, *Journal of Contemporary Issues in Business and Governance*, 4(2), 4–17.

Kouzmin, A., Rosenthal, U. and 'tHart, P. (1991) The bureau-politics of crisis management, *Public Administration*, 69(2), 211–33.

Latham, M. (2001) The network university, *Journal of Higher Education Policy and Management*, 23(1), 7–18.

McClintock, M. E. (1974) *The University of Lancaster: Quest for Innovation*. Lancaster: University of Lancaster in cooperation with Medical and Technical Publishing Co. and Construction Press.

McClintock, M. E. (1994) The University of Lancaster: the first thirty years. Lecture delivered to the Summer Programme, University of Lancaster.

Mager, C. (2002) *Taking Stock: A Review of Development in FE Colleges*. London: Learning and Skills Development Agency (LSDA).

Magretta, J. (2002) *What Is Management?* London: HarperCollins.

Martinez, P. (1994) *Research into Student Retention at Lambeth College*. Coventry: FEFC.

Martinez, P. (2000) *Raising Achievement: A Guide to Successful Strategies*. London: Department for Education and Employment.

Mitroff, I. I. (2000) *Managing Crises before They Happen: What Every Executive and Manager Needs to Know about Crisis Management*. New York: Amacom.

Monks, R. A. G. and Minow, N. (2001) *Corporate Governance*. Oxford: Blackwell.

Morgan, P. (1997) *The University of Wales 1939–1993*. Cardiff: University of Wales Press.

Muthesius, S. (2000) *The Postwar University: Utopianist Campus and College*. New Haven, CT: Paul Mellon Centre for Studies in British Art and Yale University Press.

National Assembly for Wales Education and Lifelong Learning Committee (2002) *Policy Review of Higher Education*. Cardiff: NAW.

National Audit Office (1997) *Governance and the Management of Overseas Courses at the Swansea Institute of Higher Education*. Session HC222, 1996–97, 31 January. London: HMSO.

National Audit Office (1999a) *Overseas Operations, Governance and Management at Southampton Institute*. Session 1998–1999, 26th report. London: The Stationery Office.

National Audit Office (1999b) *Managing Finances in English FE Colleges*. Session HC545, 1999. London: The Stationery Office.

National Audit Office (2001) *Improving Student Performance: How English Further Education Colleges Can Improve Student Retention and Achievement*. Session HC276, 2000–2001, 2 March. London: The Stationery Office.

Partington, P. and Stainton, C. (2003) Managing Staff Development. Maidenhead: Open University Press.

Pritchard, C. (2000) *Making Managers in Universities and Colleges*. Buckingham: Open University Press.

Public Accounts Committee (1997) *Governance and the Management of Overseas Courses at Swansea Institute of Higher Education*, 8th Report. London: HMSO.

Public Accounts Committee (1999) *Overseas Operations, Governance and Management at Southampton Institute*. Session 1998–1999, HC345, 26th Report. London: The Stationery Office.

Public Accounts Committee (2001) *Managing Finances in English Further Education Colleges*. London: The Stationery Office.

Quality Assurance Agency for Higher Education (1998) *Thames Valley University: Quality Audit Report (Special Review)*. Gloucester: QAA.

Quality Assurance Agency for Higher Education (2000) *Southampton Institute: Quality Audit Report*. Bristol: QAA.

Regester, M. and Larkin, J. (1997) *Risk Issues and Crisis Management*. London: Kogan Page.

Ritter, L. (1998) Power and perspectives: a historian's analysis of the management of change at Charles Stuart University from a federation to a centralised model, *Journal of Higher Education Policy and Management*, 20(1), 77–88.

Rosenthal, U. and Kouzmin, A. (1996) Crisis management and institutional resilience: and editorial statement, *Journal of Contingencies and Crisis Management*, 4(3), 119–24.

Rowe, P. (ed.) (1997) *Review of Institutional Lessons to Be Learned 1994–1996*. Lancaster: University of Lancaster.

Sanderson, B. (2001) *Unleashing the Tiger: Will Education and Training Transform the UK?* London: Royal Society for the Promotion of Arts and Commerce and KPMG.

Scott, P. (2000) The impact of the Research Assessment Exercise on the quality of British science and scholarship, *Anglistik*, 1, 129–43.

Selznick, P. (1957) *Leadership in Administration*. New York: Harper & Row.

Shattock, M. L. (1994) *The UGC and the Management of British Universities*. Buckingham: Society for Research into Higher Education and Open University Press.

Shattock, M. L. (2001) Review of university management and governance issues arising out of the CAPSA project, *Cambridge University Reporter*, 132(6).

Shore, C. and Wright, S. (2000) Coercive accountability: the rise of audit culture in higher education. In M. Strathern (ed.) *Audit Cultures: Anthropological Studies in Accountability, Ethics and the Academy*. London: Routledge.

Southampton Institute (2001) *Southampton Institute: Higher Education for the Modern World*. Southampton: Southampton Institute.

Standton, G. (2001) *Lessons Learned on Raising Quality and Achievement*. London: Learning and Skills Development Agency.

'tHart, P., Kouzmin, A. and Rosenthal, U. (1993) Crisis decision making: the centralization thesis revisited, *Administration and Society*, 25(1), 112–45.

Thompson, J. L. (2001) *Strategic Management*. London: Thomson Learning.

Universities and Colleges Applications Service (2002) *Applications Digest*, 19 July. Cheltenham: UCAS.

Warner, D. and Palfreyman, D. (1996) *Higher Education Management: The Key Elements*. Buckingham: Society for Research into Higher Education and Open University Press.

Warner, D. and Palfreyman, D. (eds) (2001) *The State of UK Higher Education: Managing Change and Diversity*. Buckingham: Society for Research into Higher Education and the Open University Press.

Warner, D. and Palfreyman, D. (eds) (2002) *Higher Education Law*. Bristol: Jordans.

Warner, D., Palfreyman, D. and Thomas, H. (1998) *How to Manage a Merger . . . or Avoid One*. Leeds: Heist Publications.

Watson, D. (2000) *Managing Strategy*. Buckingham: Open University Press.

Welsh Funding Council Audit Service (1997) *The Governance and Overseas Activities of Swansea Institute of Higher Education*. Cardiff: WFCAS (96/16).

INDEX

Swansea IHE, 88, 89, 98, 101
Swansea University *see* Swansea
    University
University of Western Sydney (UWS),
    academic departments, 126
    chief executive officers (CEOs), 124,
        125, 126
    communications, 128, 129, 131
    consultants, 126, 127, 129, 132
    crisis (1995), 125–6
    crisis (1999–2002), 127
    cronyism, 129
    delayering, 126
    governance, 137
    Greater Western Sydney (GWS),
        124, 129, 130
    Hawkesbury, 126
    lost opportunities, 139–40
    Macarthur, 126
    merger, 127, 136
    myths, 128
    Nepean, 125–6, 127, 135–6, 139,
        140
    partnerships, 128, 129, 133–4, 136
    publicity, 125, 127, 128, 134
    restructuring, 124–32, 134, 169
    spill-and-fill, 127
    staffing,
        morale, 128, 136
        resignations, 127, 129

strategic planning, 126–7
student numbers, 129–30
The Shape of the Future, 127, 128,
    134
trade unions, 128

value for money, 45, 143,
    149

Wales,

    see also University of Wales
    bilingualism, 96
    HEFCW *see* Higher Education
        Funding Council for Wales
    higher education institutions, 89,
        95, 96–7
    National Assembly, 97, 102
    Objective One area, 96
    tuition fees, 152
Walters, Donald, 15
Warner, David, 1–7, 88–103
Warwick University, 4, 24, 172
Welsh National School of Medicine,
    13
Wheeler, Tim, 61, 64, 66
whistle blowing, 157–8, 173
Wolverhampton University, 4

York University, 4

MANAGING EXTERNAL RELATIONS

Frank Albrighton and Julia Thomas (Eds)

Universities and colleges must pay attention to their external relations. They need good media coverage, successful fundraising, effective student recruitment and good relations with a wide range of groups. This book gives practical guidance on how to manage all areas of external relations: what to do and how to measure your success. The contributors are experienced practitioners who share their knowledge on everything from how to deal with the media to creating a web site, and from producing publications to advertising. For chief executives and senior managers, there is sound advice on how to organize the work efficiently. The world of marketing has arrived in higher education, with branding, positioning, market research and product truths now familiar concepts. The book cuts through the jargon and provides usable advice in an informed and informal way.

Contents
Preface – What is external relations for? – A rose by any other name: brand management and visual identity – So that's what they think: market research – Impress to print: publications – Commercial breaks: a planned approach to advertising – Casting your net: the internet and its role in university marketing – 'Happy Days' or 'Nightmare on Fleet Street'?: media relations – Why aren't we speaking to each other?: internal communications – Guess who's coming to dinner?: event management – What are friends for?: alumni relations – Money, money, money: managing the fundraising process – Well connected: organizational structure – All together now: a strategic institutional approach to integrated marketing – A seat at the table: performance measurement – Appendices – Bibliography – Index.

192pp   0 335 20789 8 (Paperback)   0 335 20790 1 (Hardback)

HIGHER EDUCATION MANAGEMENT
THE KEY ELEMENTS

David Warner and David Palfreyman (Eds.)

Many higher education institutions are like small towns, meeting the needs of their members by providing not only specialist teaching and research activities but also residential accommodation, catering, telecommunications, counselling, sports facilities and so on. The management of these institutions is very complex, requiring both generalist and specialist knowledge and skills; and the move to formal strategic planning means that it is no longer acceptable for higher education managers to be aware only of their own relatively narrow areas of expertise. All new managers would benefit from an holistic perspective on managing a whole institution. As such individuals are promoted, such 'helicopter vision' becomes a precondition of their and their institution's success. *Higher Education Management* provides:

- the first comprehensive account of non-academic higher education management;
- contributions from distinguished practitioners of university management;
- a key resource for all aspiring, trainee and practising managers in higher education.

Contents
Setting the scene – Organizational culture – Strategic planning – Sources of funds and resource allocation – Financial management – Decision-making and committees – Personnel management – Student management – Post-graduate and research organization and management – Estate management – Campus support services – Student support services – External relations – Academic support services – Management student learning – Notes on the legal framework within which HEIs operate – Notes of further reading – Bibliography – Index.

256pp   0 335 19569 5 (Paperback)   0 335 19570 9 (Hardback)